I BELIEVE IN MISSION

I BELIEVE
IN MISSION

by

CUTHBERT BARDSLEY

Bishop of Coventry

'. . . proclaim the message,
press it home on all occasions.'
2 Tim. 4.2

LONDON

A. R. MOWBRAY & CO LTD

First published in 1970

© *Cuthbert Bardsley 1970*

SBN 264 64515 4

Made in Great Britain at the Pitman Press, Bath

ACKNOWLEDGEMENTS

THE THANKS of the author and publishers are due to the following for permission to reproduce copyright material:

Cambridge University Press, for two extracts from the *New English Bible*; Gill and Macmillan Ltd., for an extract from *Prayers of Life*, by Michel Quoist; Hodder and Stoughton, for an extract from *Bury Me in My Boots*, by Sally Trench; Inter-Varsity Press, for an extract from *Man Alive*, by Michael Green.

The author is also grateful to the under-mentioned people for their kind permission to reproduce, either in whole or in part, the talks and personal statements of faith which they made during the Call to Mission: The Archbishop of York; Cliff Richard; Tom Coyne; Dr. Leslie Davison; Derek Nimmo; The Rt. Hon. Quintin Hogg; Colin Cowdrey; Andrew Cruickshank; Lady Chichester; Mrs. Joanna Kelley; Lord Carron; Mrs. Margaret Gillespie; Lewis J. Davey, John S. Haynes; Sister Peggy Boynes, C.A.; Peter Worsley; Stephen Arnold; Mrs. L. Davis; Mr. Tom Shepherd; Stuart Bell; Mrs. Beryl Evans; Mr. G. W. Sanders.

Contents

Author's Foreword

IT IS inevitable, because this book is concerned with a mission which was associated with my name, that people will tend to think of it as an individual effort of my own. But nothing could be further from the truth.

Nothing of the Coventry Mission could have happened but for the devoted service of a group of people whom I wish to mention by name. These include Canon Geoffrey Rogers, the Diocesan Missioner who was mainly responsible for the training of the seven hundred who sought to be prepared for counselling. All of these people paid tribute to the excellence of his teaching.

Next, I would like to thank Mr. Lewis Davey, my Personal Assistant, who gave constant and vigilant care in the preparations for the Mission, not least in acting as Treasurer, and for the trouble that he has subsequently taken in going through the proofs of my addresses for this book. The whole-time secretary of the Call to Mission was the Reverend Peter Larkin, a young priest in my diocese who, eighteen months before it began, left his parish to take over the immense job of preparation for this enterprise. I cannot speak sufficiently highly of the excellence of his work and of his efficiency. Mr. John Haynes was placed in charge of publicity and did a magnificent piece of work in preparing posters, car-stickers, in the use of space in local papers, and in all the work associated with publicity of the project.

I am also deeply indebted to Canon Lawrence Jackson, Vicar of Holy Trinity, Coventry, for acting as compère, night by night throughout the Mission. For his humour and his enthusiasm I am indeed greatly in his debt. Finally I would like to make appreciative reference to the

Reverend Kingsley Walker and to Sister Peggy Boynes of the Church Armies. The former did excellent work in going around the parishes speaking about the Mission, and in preparing clergy and lay people for it; the latter did valiant work in heading the Mission Office Staff. To her, and to the voluntary part-time and whole time workers who came in large numbers to man the office, I shall always feel deeply grateful.

But at the very outset of this book I want to make it quite clear that I am not so naive as to imagine that the kind of mission outlined in these pages is the only valid kind. Mission takes many and various forms. Sometimes, and maybe increasingly these days, it takes the form of personal dialogue through meetings in homes and through discussions with seekers after the faith. Sometimes mission takes the form of encounter with people through personal service, when Christians can be asked why they do what they do, and why they conduct themselves as they do. Mission, indeed, can take the form of seeking for opportunities, in service of others, for saying something, in deed as well as in word, about Christian motivation. But sometimes mission takes the form of proclamation, by one or more people, of their understanding of the Christian faith, leading men to accept or to reject what that faith which has been proclaimed stands for.

It is this third kind of mission which is the concern of this book. It is sometimes said that the day of this sort of mission is over. I do not believe this to be the case, and I hope that when people have read this book they will feel that, provided there has been careful preparation over a long period of time, and provided there is an equally careful follow-up, there is still a place for the kind of proclamation of the Christian faith such as is narrated in these pages.

CUTHBERT COVENTRY

I

Background to a Mission

THE COVENTRY MISSION, or 'Call to Mission' as it was named at the time because it is to be understood as the beginning of a continuing mission, reached its high point, in terms of intensity of effort and of public proclamation of the Gospel, between the 17th and the 27th of September, 1968, culminating in a great open-air diocesan eucharist on the following Sunday. Before those dates, however, very much had happened in terms of preparation, and since those dates very much has happened in the way of follow-up. This book, although it appears a considerable time after the centre-point of the mission, does so when it is at last possible, as it were, to recollect emotion in tranquility, and to survey the whole field of this particular mission enterprise both as regards what took place before, and what is still taking place afterwards. In this manner, and in this manner only, is it possible to evaluate an undertaking of this sort. Many lessons were learned in the course of it; and the actual carrying through of a mission, with all which it involved both before and after, is in itself a valuable, indeed essential, preliminary to reaching any conclusions about the place of mission in the Christian scheme today. It is therefore the case that, though much of this book is occupied with what was actually said in

Coventry Cathedral on the eleven nights of the central part of the mission, it is also possible now to set something down regarding these general conclusions about mission today and also to say something, at the end of the book, about what has happened subsequently.

What, for instance, should be the structure of mission nowadays? The Gospel, of course, is the same in all ages; but the manner of its presentation changes from time to time. Furthermore, different generations require different emphases. This generation is rightly conscious of the wonder of the humility and outgoing service of the incarnate Christ—the man for others. Young people particularly are deeply exercised by the inequalities of society, especially those between East and West; they are exercised by the moral and physical threats of nuclear warfare; they are exercised, and rightly so, by many of those elements in modern society which show it to be far from what it could be or should be in so technologically rich an age as the present. Furthermore, anything which savours of condescension is to them suspect, I would say that the facet of our Lord's character which appeals most to the young is his humility and outgoing service.

It therefore follows that in our evangelism the Gospel, or so it seems to me, must be expressed in and through service, and at least those who preach the Gospel must be seen to be also deeply involved in outgoing service to the community. We must not give the impression of isolated, separatist church-filling, but rather of humble, devoted selfless service of others. Emotional hymns may not appeal to the younger generation; but teaching such as that of Matthew 25 is very much respected and admired, once it is explained. Action appeals to this generation more than words. But words have their place also. The preacher will still be listened to, provided he is in a setting of service.

But what he says must be open-ended: there must be opportunities for come-back, for question and answer, for dialogue and criticism. The great 'Establishment' utterance is suspect. The 'take-it-or-leave-it' pronouncement falls on deaf or, more often, rebellious ears. The saints these days are those who are seen to be most deeply involved in sacrificial service to the community. But any authoritarian pronouncement which is not backed up by reasoned argument does not stand a chance.

Does this mean, then, that the old methods of proclamation through sermons and parochial mission are finished? Personally, I believe that they still have their place provided that they emerge from and through visible long-term humble service; that they are accompanied by a visible willingness to be open to argument and criticism.

The best, in the sense of the most effective, missions are those held within the setting of parish neighbourhood or diocese, and then only after a long period of visible service and identification by the Church with the needs of the surrounding community. The professional evangelist coming in from outside is suspect these days. People prefer their own man, who is known to be and seen to be involved in their own problems and concerns. I truly believe that people would rather have their own local 'evangelist' with all his limitations, than, nowadays, any 'expert' brought in from outside.

In a Methodist pamphlet on evangelism which I have read since the Coventry Call to Mission, it was suggested that an evangelistic campaign should be conducted in three parts, taking in all about eighteen months. The first part, called the Initiation Campaign, should have as its objective the preparation of the local church community. This, in fact, is exactly what happened in Coventry on the occasion of our Call to Mission, which took as its starting point the fact of the fiftieth anniversary of the foundation of the diocese. Workshops were formed in parish and rural deaneries to study the Bible, prayer and witness. Then ensued a period of intensive training of those willing to be Counsellors. This training, largely centred in Bible teaching, lasted three months. As a result, although seven hundred began the course, only three hundred were accepted at the end as Counsellors, a fact which gives some idea of the rigour of the training and of the standard demanded. Agents were appointed throughout the diocese to cover prayer, house-to-house visiting, publicity, transport and youth. The result of all this long preparation, even in this first stage alone, was that before the Mission began several clergy said that it would have been worth while, even if no actual mission had been held, if only for the spiritual gains which had arisen from the period of preparation.

The Methodist pamphlet on evangelism also advocated a second stage called the Acceleration Campaign. Here again, the Coventry procedure was similar. The second stage of our preparations took the form of house-to-house visitation, and every house in many parishes was visited by a team of lay visitors. It also took the form of intensive, widespread and professionally prepared advertising over a period of weeks, and finally took the form of home meetings for discussion, witness, and the study of the Gospel.

The third part of the preparation campaign advocated in the Methodist pamphlet is there given the name of a Realisation Campaign. It is in this final stage that mission moves to evangelism. The aim is to bring all the local programmes to a climax in which people are led to a point of decision and to specific commitment to Christ and to service throughout the Church. The dominant feature of this phase is preaching. Here again this happened in our Coventry Mission. There were indeed eleven nights of preaching, and of the giving of witness by lay people. What happened on those nights, and what was said on those nights, is set forth in detail in the later pages of this book. But it is important that this part of the Mission should not be seen in isolation; but that these prolonged and intensive periods and forms of preparation should constantly be kept in mind. The evangelistic addresses, when it thus came to the time to give them, in the third stage of the Mission, were presented under the overall title of 'Learn to Live'. The meetings were held in the Cathedral, at Coventry, and were linked by closed-circuit television, projected on giant screens, to other centres, including a neighbouring parish church, a neighbouring college of technology and the Methodist Central Hall, generously and eagerly placed at our disposal. The closed-circuit television, although it was extremely expensive, amply justified itself and made possible an extension of the audience which would not otherwise have been practicable. There were never less than two thousand people present on any night of this preaching part of the Mission, and on the Youth Night the figures reached seven thousand, five hundred.

But—and this I would emphasise—the purpose of this long and careful three-phase campaign was to ensure that as wide a body of people as possible were trained, and that the evangelistic campaign should be seen as only part of an on-going mission, and that the whole thing should be recognised not as an isolated ten-day venture, but as part of the Church's on-going mission to the community.

There is always a danger, today, that the emphasis on

Christian service to the community should push evangelism, in a sense of the proclamation of the Gospel, to the circumference, and that a religion of works will supersede a religion of faith. The approach to the Kingdom of God will be thought to be by our own works, rather than by God's works. It follows, therefore, that preaching must be incarnated in the flesh and blood of humble personal service; but preaching there must be. Nonetheless, as I have said, the proclaiming Church must be the serving Church; but it must also be the proclaiming Church.

Evangelism must be seen, too, in its widest setting, as an expression of the whole family of God and not as one small part of it. It is true that the Coventry 'Call to Mission' largely owing to its historical starting point in the fiftieth anniversary of the foundation of the diocese, was an Anglican undertaking. But there seems little reason to doubt that an ecumenical mission is all the stronger for being so, whenever it is possible. Ecumenism is in our bones today. Evangelism is not the private possession of different churches any longer; but rather must be seen to be part of the general on-going work of all the churches acting together. This ecumenical outlook is part of the general outlook of the world today. It lies behind the ideas of those who believe in a supra-racial family, one family of whatever colour or background which shall at last learn to inhabit the earth in peace. This is an idea which appeals, and rightly so, very strongly indeed to the young. Obviously, ecumenism in evangelism is bound to give rise to difficulties. It is hard enough to implement evangelism on the denominational basis. It is ten times harder to plan it ecumenically. And yet I believe it must, where possible, be done. But if it is to be done, the three-fold phasing of a campaign, such as I have been speaking of, will still be applicable. The only difference is

6

that it would take longer. The eighteen months preparation may well take three years. But the value of an
ecumenic evangelistic campaign is incalculable. When
people see Christians of different denominations proclaiming the Gospel together, the result will be immensely
more effective than otherwise it might be. Also, team
planning of any ecumenical mission must be united in
terms of the persons engaged in it. They must live together, pray together, work together over a long period,
and always trust one another implicitly and together
wait upon the Lord in the spirit. Everything that is good
emerges from teams of united, fearless, and God-filled
people. Even so, it must always be remembered that
ecumenical mission will not just happen because somebody has a good idea, or because somebody thinks it will
be a good thing. It will be born and emerge and develop
through the team of people who love and trust each other,
who are loving, honest and trenchant with one another;
who are seen by the community and society to be truly
united in love, and to be expressing that love in practice.

The matter of lay participation in mission is also of
great importance. Gone are the days of missions run
exclusively by the clergy. Gone are the days of missions
run by one great and famous missioner, as I have said.
There may still be a place for people like Dr. Billy
Graham, to whose excellent work in years past I would
pay tribute; but it must never be forgotten that the
preparation for his comings have been carefully prepared
by many lay people over a long period in each instance.
My own deep conviction is that effective evangelistic
mission depends almost entirely upon the adequate
training of a very large number of lay people with a deep
and personal knowledge of the Gospel, who are able,
intelligently and powerfully, to communicate it.

By the time the Coventry Mission began we had over seven hundred people who had been through intensive training in the difficult art of communicating the Gospel to others. And in the actual programme each night of the mission lay people played an important and effective role. Furthermore, eighteen months before the mission proper began, every parish in the diocese had appointed seven lay people to be in charge of prayer groups, of house-to-house visitation, of publicity, finance, transport and so forth. Without these lay people, carefully trained, and setting aside a great deal of time and thought, I am quite sure that our mission would not have been anything like as effective as it was. I see no reason why this lay training should not be done, as I have tried to say, ecumenically together. I am also convinced that nowadays the laity are more anxious for mission and for united and ecumenical action than, in many cases, are the clergy. And so the laity will prod, stir and stimulate us into action and unless we listen to their pleading and act upon their desires, there is always the possibility that they will take the matter into their own hands and initiate action themselves.

Another lesson which was taught us all, I think, by the Coventry Call to Mission, was the importance of publicity through radio, television and Press coverage. We were greatly helped before and during the mission by BBC radio and television. Sound radio carried a series of pre-mission talks, in which I was privileged to address a national audience. On television there were two programmes, including a magnificent coverage of the final eucharist, which was also televised on the national network of the BBC. As to publicity within the area of the mission itself, it is important to note that a professional was asked to take over all the publicity prior to the mission. This he did brilliantly, taking an increasing amount of space in local papers, devising first-class pamphlets and posters, and generally making people aware of what was about to take place. I cannot speak too strongly of the necessity for professional handling of this means of publicity—and indeed of any other. Of course, it is costly. But as a result, at any rate in our case, many hundreds of people came to the mission—possibly many thousands, who would not otherwise have been present, or even have heard of it.

And now a word about the preaching itself. The purpose of evangelism, however it is devised, is still to bring people to a point of decision and to specific commitment to Christ and to service of him through the Church. It follows that regular opportunity should be provided for the public demonstration of decision or profession of faith. Opportunity should be given for those who desire to re-dedicate themselves and to renew their vows, or for young people making their first decision to follow Christ, or for those who are approaching the Church for the first time, or for those who need the grace of forgiveness and renewal of hope, to come at these things. It is at this point, it seems to me, that the actual preaching should be handed over to one man who shall, to the best of his ability, and by virtue of his office, declare the faith in positive terms which lead to decision and commitment. This is a neglected ministry in the Church today and one that is somewhat disparaged. This may well be partly due to the fact that in the past it has been misused, taking the form of attempts to brainwash people into an emotional state with the intention of getting a decision at almost any cost. Such forms of mental and emotional coercion, or of the presentation of the Gospel in a way that violates the sacred preserve and privacy of personality, are indeed much to be criticised. It is also true that the preaching of the Gospel evangelistically is open to many dangers. Nevertheless, the Church desperately needs evangelists today who, while cautious of emotionalism, are not afraid of emotion. For we must realise that because the Gospel speaks to the whole man, it is not properly preached unless the whole man is reached. This means touching the deep chords of feeling. Far too often in teaching we bring people to the place where they are deeply moved; but do not provide opportunities for them to express their feeling in decision leading to commitment and action. I know very many people now in my own diocese who, as a result of a decision they made during one of the evenings of the mission, have been very different people since, and have indeed been, I think it is not too much to say, brought to Christ. Not the least of the advantages of bringing out a book like this so long after the event, is that it is possible to say such things as that in the knowledge that they have happened, and that the changes in these people have stood the test of time.

In all that I have been saying so far I have been using three terms fairly loosely: mission, evangelism and Gospel. It might well be advisable, at this stage, to be more precise. Mission obviously has its roots in the idea of being sent; evangelism takes us on to the fact that we are sent with a message. We are left with the question: what is the message? It is my belief that we have over-complicated this whole matter and made many people think that the Gospel is, as it were, a complex matter within the reach of only the instructed few. Surely this is entirely untrue. It is certainly not the message which our Lord brought to the people of Galilee and Jerusalem, and which was conveyed by the early Church to a world in which it was heard gladly.

The essence of the Gospel message is that God is, that

God loves, and that Christ saves. Elaborations and permutations of this are virtually endless. But these are the basic elements of it. And, right at the heart of this, is something which modern man, whether old or young, in whatever situation he may be, quite desperately, in my view, in these days needs not only to know, but to feel and accept. He needs to know and to feel and to accept that he is not alone in what appears to be an impersonal universe; but that he is in fact a creature of God, known to God, loved by God and accountable to God. This, it seems to me, is the Gospel: this is the good news. It staggers and amazes me that this good news is not more often heard and not more often proclaimed. This Gospel message, moreover, demands a verdict. We cannot forever continue to proclaim such a message, without at the same time expecting that people will either accept or reject it. But nowadays people are either ignoring it, or never hearing it. In the early days of the Church, it was not considered odd that an address should elicit the response: 'Men and brethren, what shall we do?' But how seldom is that response expected or expressed now!

We may take it as an ancient truth that the validity of any spiritual response can be tested by the change of life to which it gives rise, and this also, in the teaching of the Gospel, must be made plain. We are to preach the new man in Christ. Such, now as ever, is part of the Christian task, and it involves asking people whether they are prepared to put their lives at the disposal of Christ. To this they can give a 'yes', or they can give a 'no'. But they should be given the opportunity of saying one or the other.

There remains the very important question of the follow-up to any mission enterprise. In all preparations for a mission very careful thought must be given, long before it begins, to the whole matter of this follow up. In the case of the Coventry Call to Mission, we began to think about the follow-up months before the whole thing began. And, since the enterprise itself, I have rejoiced to see this follow-up expressing itself among clergy and laity. To my great joy clergy have expressed a great longing for training in theology, in sociology, in spirituality and in evangelism. Very many have, as a result of the Call to Mission, begun to realise how little they have read in recent years, how lacking is their knowledge of contemporary theology, how thin is their understanding of recent theological developments. They have as a result expressed a great desire to study and to sit at the feet of theological experts in order that they may be the more effective in communicating the Gospel more intelligently to the world of today. A number have also expressed their keen desire to understand their surrounding community, and to come to grips with what is going on in modern society. As a result, they have entered into sociological studies and are profiting much therefrom. But perhaps the most interesting development of all has been an almost passionate desire on the part of some clergy to have a deepened spirituality. These realised that the one thing that is needed is holiness, and they have been made aware by the 'Call to Mission', in many cases, how shallow their spirituality has been. One result has been a widespread desire not only to learn more about prayer, but to express it more effectively; not only to learn more about the Bible; but to meditate upon it; not only to learn more about contemporary forms of worship; but to experience this worship deeply in their own lives.

There have been clergy also, who have realised how ineffective, in many cases, has been their own evangelism, and they have desired to find how they could remedy this. All this adds up, on the part of some of the clergy, to a reawakening of the whole personality, to the revival of the true ministry of those involved. This continues to be a matter for very great rejoicing.

Among the laity, I have found that, almost universally, among the many hundreds of lay people who have met together following on the Call to Mission, there has been, and continues to be, almost universal recognition of the barrenness of their prayer life, of their failure to understand the teaching of the Bible. With this has come a passionate desire to have clear and simple teaching on prayer, and to meet together in groups of praying people, and to have Bible instruction and to meet together as groups wrestling with God's message through his word. I have also seen many lay people meeting together in house groups, under one another's roofs; not listening to lectures so much as in dialogue with each other finding a deepened understanding of the faith.

In all that I have been saying it may have appeared that I have been speaking and thinking perhaps excessively about evangelism as it concerns those within reach of the Church, and that I have been giving too little time in talking about mission to the great unchurched—the vast majority of our population today. This may have been so. But I make no apology for this. After all, Paul's evangelism was very largely directed at the people within his own Church—the people of Israel or, later, with people who were interested in religious matters. And surely he was right. He saw his task as the quickening, the bringing alive of the faithful or of the seekers. They would then become the missioners to the great unchurched. And so it has been throughout the centuries. The great unchurched masses will sit up and take notice when they see the Church being the Church and proclaiming the Gospel with power and with 'signs following'. When they see church people filled with joyful and infectious holiness; when they see the Church itself deeply concerned about the surrounding community and expressing itself continually in active out-going and humble service, then they will take notice. The living Church, the Church alive unto God—the Church alive to her responsibilities for mission—the Church will be the spearhead of evangelism. But it will do it mainly, as I have said, in the setting of service: in the setting of the workaday world, doing it day by day through compassion, through attractive holiness, through speaking of the Gospel.

Meanwhile, the Church's job is to create these missionaries. And once the missionary has become alive unto God, nothing will keep him from communicating his faith. The fire of his personal experience will spread to others. So I do not apologise for appearing to concentrate more on the faithful and the fringer than on the total outsider, because it is with the faithful and the fringer that evangelism begins and continues. May God help us all to discover how to bring the Church alive unto God, so that the world may sit up and take notice and accept Jesus Christ as Saviour and Lord.

2

The Scene of the Mission

THE Coventry Call to Mission reached its high point, in terms of intensity of effort and of public proclamation of the Gospel, between the 17th and the 27th September, 1968. Before that, however, very long, carefully-planned and extensive preparation took place. Similarly, since then, a great deal has happened and continues to happen up to this present moment, as a sequel or, as I would prefer to call it 'The continuing task'. It would be very far from my intentions, or indeed from the truth, to represent these gatherings in Coventry Cathedral on those eleven evenings in September as in themselves the mission. They were part of it only, and it would be both a travesty of the truth and a serious misrepresentation of the facts as well as the giving of a false idea of mission to represent that series of gatherings as in any way the totality of the mission in the minds of those who were concerned with it, and who have continued to be concerned with it since.

Nonetheless, those eleven evenings in that September were memorable indeed. It seems proper, therefore, since so much of this book is concerned with what was said by various persons on those evenings, to try to recapture some of the scene and the atmosphere before passing on to the record of some of what was said.

But the persons deeply involved in such an enterprise are not necessarily the best persons to give an impartial description of the scene as it has implanted itself in the memory. Because of that fact, I have asked one who was present, as an observer only, at most of the evenings of this part of the Call to Mission, to describe the scene and the sequence of events as he saw them, and what follows is his account.

'Coventry Cathedral, as so many know, is an impressive building at any time. On these particular evenings of the mission, when it was filled not only with people, but also with a sense of expectancy, it was impressive indeed. Seen from the back of the building, the congregation, nearly always during these evenings very large, seemed dwarfed by the towering Christ figure in the tapestry dominating the eastern end of the Cathedral. Before the High Altar, the black marble chancel had been extended at its western end by a platform, carefully spot-lit, upon which the speakers took their stand and from which, on most occasions, the musicians performed. The music throughout the nights of the mission was of a wide variety. On one evening it might be a West Indian family, The Singing Stuarts, whose music seemed to combine to an extraordinary degree conviction with gaiety: on another occasion it might be the Coventry Salvation Army band, on another the singing of Mr. Owen Brannigan, on another the trumpet of Mr. Roy Castle, on another the music of the pop group known as The Settlers. It was noticeable on all these gatherings that one of the first, and yet often overlooked essentials of public communication had received careful attention—the sound—was excellent, and everyone could hear, whether speech or song.

A television camera on a platform to the left of the chancel steps, and another at the rear of the building were reminders that the proceedings were being covered by closed-circuit television and could be seen and heard by other large audiences in the neighbouring parish church of Holy Trinity, in the Lanchester College of Technology, over the way from the Cathedral, and in the Methodist Central Hall some little distance away across the town. In many ways indeed, a more intimate view of the speaker was to be had in th⁄ se overflow gatherings than in the Cathedral itself. The large screen showed him in close-up in a manner in which it was not possible for the human eye to encompass in the Cathedral itself, and this gave a degree of intimacy and communication with the speaker which was always impressive and, at times, moving. What the television cameras could not show, however, were other intimacies of these gatherings: the expressions on the faces of the audience among them. These were at times a fascinating human study, ranging from placidity to intense attention; sometimes to dis-approval, sometimes, it seemed, to surprise at what was being said and done and, not infrequently, to deep emotion. Those who stayed behind at the Bishop's invitation at the close of each meeting in order that, as he often put it, "they may do their business with God" were, naturally enough, not televised.

The order of events on each evening appeared to be informal enough. It soon became apparent, however, that in fact a carefully-prepared pattern was being followed. Always, each evening, there was a period of "warm-up" in which Canon Lawrence Jackson, Vicar of the neighbouring church of Holy Trinity, acted as compère, leading the congregation in the programme of hymn-singing and clearly helping them to settle down and relax. This was done with great skill and could, without that skill, quite obviously have been disastrous. In fact, it appeared to work very well and to achieve its object. This would last for something like half an hour before the actual programme of the evening began. This programme usually, in addition to its musical content, included two speakers who came on before the Bishop entered to give the main address of the evening. These two preliminary speakers, on most evenings, were of two kinds: the known and the unknown. One of them, that is to say, was usually a well-known public figure, in some cases of much distinction: the other would be a man or woman from the diocese of Coventry who had, in some cases clearly with much trepidation and steeling of the will to the challenge, come out of private life to stand up and give a personal testimony as to what their faith had meant to them. The combination of these two kinds of persons was, whether by accident or design, highly effective. The very fact that both were speaking about the same faith and about what it had meant to them, and was continuing to mean to them, was a powerful testimony to the universality and power of that faith. And the fact that many of the speakers came from varying Christian communions added to the power and range of their messages.

As to the nature of these audiences at these mission gatherings, it would seem impossible to generalise. All that can perhaps be said is that there appeared to be all kinds and conditions of people present: men and women, young and old, from across the whole spectrum of society. How many lives were touched; how many untouched; in how many cases the seed fell on stony ground; in how many cases it fell on good ground and bore fruit a thousandfold, are questions no doubt for God rather than for man. At any event, they evade an answer. One fact which appeared inescapable to the observer was that many who came to watch remained to pray, and that a great many seemed to go away into the September nights again impressed and moved.'

3

The Message of the Mission - Learn to Live

As HAS been stated in that observer's account, on most nights of the Call to Mission there were speakers who came before the main address of the evening in each instance. In some cases they were interviewed, the interviewers being Mr. Tom Coyne, of the BBC, Mr. Wynford Vaughan-Thomas, Canon Geoffrey Rogers, Coventry Diocesan Missioner, the Rev. Peter Larkin, a clergyman on the mission staff, the Rev. John Moore, Youth Chaplain to the Coventry Diocese, and Mr. Ronald Allison of the BBC. In other instances they were not interviewed; but made their personal statements direct. In what follows here in this book these statements are given in extract, condensed to give the essence of what each speaker said, with matters of temporary and local relevance removed. Similarly, in the case of those who were interviewed, the interviewer's participation has been omitted as not strictly relevant, and the gist of the speaker's own statement preserved.

THE ARCHBISHOP OF YORK

The Archbishop of York, the Most Reverend and Right Honourable F. D. Coggan, launched the Call to Mission with a brief ceremony on the opening night at which he lit, outside the Cathedral, the torches which were used throughout the mission as sign and symbol of its nature. It is to these torches that the Archbishop makes reference in his opening words.

I want very briefly to take up the theme that we kindled symbolically tonight, and I want to tell you very simply what Jesus Christ, the Light of the World, has meant to me down the years, and what he means to me today. . . . I find, first of all, that Jesus Christ sheds a light on the problem that is 'me' and that's quite a problem, for everyone of us is an extraordinary bundle of possibilities for good or bad—a bundle of passions that need controlling. We are a bundle of ambitions, some of which are good, some of which are bad and he is a foolish man or woman who does not sooner or later—the sooner the better—try to find an answer to the question—'What am I?' Am I simply an animal at the top of the animal grade, or am I a son of God, a daughter of God in the making. Christ says I am the latter, and he is here to make me what potentially I am, and all he asks is a chance to get busy on that big operation. So I say thank God for Jesus Christ, who sheds a light on the primary problem, which is me.

I have a word of advice for you tonight: if you wish it easy in the years ahead I would not come back to these meetings, because there is a risk in coming back to these meetings—the risk is that if you are not already an active Christian, you will be one by the end of these days. And if you do become an active Christian in the next ten days —and indeed many of you will—you will automatically become a world citizen because you will be following the Saviour of the world, and once you begin to follow him you necessarily have a share in the griefs and sorrows of this torn world. The world, a large part of which is on the starvation line, a large part of which is illiterate, a large part of which is in the throes of a domination over which it has no control.

Now the redemption of that world cost God his son, and therefore if I am in any technical sense a servant of that God, his world is my world, and I am in with him on the fight to redeem that world. And that will cost and that will hurt. So, listen to my advice; if you want it easy do not come back because Christ has a way of shedding an uneasy light on the world I live in. But, of course, if you do not share it with him you miss the fight and you miss the fun and you miss the pain. Christ, who is the Light of the World, sheds a light on the world. I have hosts of questions and answers about what happens when this little span of life is over, as it will be very shortly. But this I know: Christ our Lord went through the gate of death and rose victorious, and in that going through and in that rising he brought life and immortality to life by the Gospel.

And so I know that he lives, and so I know that he reigns, and so I can say that part of the Creed with deep conviction which says, 'I believe in the forgiveness of sins, and I believe in the life of the world to come.' Now I say, thank God for Christ who lights up the problem—me, the world of which I am a part, the world to which I go. It does not solve all my problems. I have no facile Gospel for you. Discipleship of Jesus Christ creates a host of problems of which you know nothing until you become a Christian. It does not give you a key that automatically unlocks the lock: it does not give you a bed of roses to lie on. But, Christ gives you his hand and he gives you a torch, enough strength to go on and enough light to walk by.

This is going to be the centre of the Bishop's message night after night in the Cathedral, and throughout this diocese and away beyond. And you will listen and you will obey, and you will see Christ as not only the Light of the World in some vague way, but as your life and as your salvation. And in that light of life you will walk until travelling days are done. God bless you all.

STEPHEN ARNOLD
A PERSONAL STATEMENT

Stephen Arnold was an ex-miner, out of work at the time of the Call to Mission. He is now training to be a youth leader.

I was brought up by my parents who were concerned for me and desired I should learn more of the knowledge and the love of God, and accept him as my master. I was confirmed when I was quite young and I did not fully understand the promise I had made. I was eighteen when I realised I was playing around with Christianity and had to accept God as my master. I was helped considerably by week-ends and adventure courses organised by the diocese and especially holidays organised by the Youth

Chaplain. It was here that I realised there was a purpose to life, and that we all have our part to play, no matter what our intellect or abilities are.

A small youth group was formed after one such holiday, in Coventry, and here it was that I learned how similar young people had the same doubts and difficulties as myself, and we were able to discuss our problems and be helped by other people's knowledge and love of God. I realised the need for daily prayer and Bible study to be in conversation with God. I am now only twenty-one and in that comparatively short time have found a far deeper understanding and love of our Lord. But no matter what our upbringing was, or is, it still remains that *I* have to make the decision—it has to be a personal response to God. My parents or friends could not make it for me. The decision was mine.

Since then I have been made redundant from a colliery, and have realised that as a Christian it's not simply plain sailing and easy going. God does make demands on my life and has asked me to do things I felt incapable of doing. But with his strength and power I have found them possible, and a far deeper faith in doing them.

* * *

The First Talk
LEARN TO LIVE WITH YOURSELF

I ask forgiveness in advance for what may be very halting words from one who is by no means a 'professional' Evangelist, but one who just loves his Lord and longs that every man, woman and child shall come to know the

Lord Jesus Christ as their personal Saviour, Master and Lord.

As I look out upon you all—and I am told there are well over five and a half thousand people here—I realise that, if there is one thing common to all of us it is that we live in a world that is both exciting and dangerous. I want to make it very clear that this Call to Mission is not an escape from that exciting and dangerous world; but is intended to be rather the opportunity for a meeting with the Lord who calls us to serve him in the world, exciting and dangerous as it may be.

I have used the word 'exciting' of this world. I could also have used the word 'changeful'. It is science and technology, largely, which have changed our world so much. Space research has set man on his way, in physical fact, to the planets. Atomic energy has brought us to the threshold of an industrial revolution which will make the first revolution look tame. It has been said that more change has taken place in the last thirty years than in the previous thousand years of man's history. A host of other breaks-through have brought the possibility of a greater freedom from the physical limitations of life in the material world than has been possible for any previous generation. All that is one side of the coin—the bright and glittering side. But there is another. It is a darker one. We know it well: for in its darkness lurk many of the sombre facts of our life—racial tensions of the gravest sort; wars and rumours of wars; and famine and undernourishment in nearly half the world's population. And it is a known fact that emotional, mental and nervous disorders, part of the price of our high-speed world, are widespread.

A friend of mine in the United States some years ago saw a notice outside a church. At first sight, what he read might appear, when quoted, to be a cheap joke. In fact, it contained a profound truth, which is why I mention it now. The notice read: 'Preacher next Sunday, the Rev. So-and-So. Subject of his address: "What's Wrong with the World?" Words of the anthem: "Search me, O God".' I believe that, quite simply and basically, that is where we have to begin, with ourselves, if ever we are to try to face up constructively to the manifold problems of the dark side of life. For it is a fact that the trouble with the world is the people living in it. Obviously, they are complex in origin and effect. There are basic flaws in systems of government; power structures are dangerous; mass media of communications can be corrupting; an economic system which permits one half of the world to live in luxury and the other half in poverty is clearly out of order. Yet, basically, the root trouble is to be found in man himself. Man is born with limitless possibilities for good but, as an observable fact of experience, he is too often corrupt, selfish, grasping, greedy, and cruel. And here we are confronted with two further basic facts; first, that we could never get away from ourselves, ever. Whatever we do, wherever we go, we are ourselves forever. Unaided, we can never, what is more, refashion our characters, or iron out of them the fundamental predispositions towards evil which lurk within us all. Only the power of God revealed in Jesus Christ can do that. Of that there will be much—very much—more to be said as this mission progresses.

But just now, let me ask this. Who and what is this self —this individual self, from which none of us can escape? Some hold the view that a human being is made of a sum total of its perishable tissues; occupying so much space, a body to be fed and kept warm—and that is all. But we know in our hearts that this is not so. The yearnings, the questionings, the joys and sorrows which go to make up the still, sad music of humanity cannot be explained away on such a shallow basis as that. Nor are we computers. The one thing a computer cannot do is to answer the question 'What is a computer?' Nor are we what we are solely because of hereditary factors beyond our control or choice. Nor are we, in our responses to life, in the shape of our personalities and actions, the products solely of environment.

When we are honest, we know that these are evasions. Recently I read a book by a girl called Sally Trench: *Bury Me in My Boots*[1]. It is the story of a seventeen year old girl, brought up in a rich home. With all that money could buy, she yet suddenly decided to discover how the other part of the world—the dark side of it—lived. She started in London's Piccadilly, among the drop-outs. From there she progressed, if that is the word, to meths. drinkers and drug addicts. Four years she worked among these people, sometimes, but by no means always, succeeding in breaking through to a genuine human contact. If this girl has been merely the result of heredity or environment she would never have acted thus. Every element in her background would have urged her against it. Yet, in the event, the effort and the action were extraordinary, heroic, and in ordinary human terms, inexplicable.

The relevance of this story to what I am trying to say is that this girl had found the true answer to the problem of living with herself by forgetting herself in selfless service. This is the true answer, and I shall have more to say of it later in these talks when I shall be speaking of living for others. But, for the moment, let us look at some false answers which people sometimes arrive at in trying to solve the problem of living with themselves.

One false illusion is to devote life to the wrong ends,

[1] Sally Trench, *Bury Me in My Boots*. Hodder and Stoughton.

and by wrong I mean ends which are ultimately false and valueless. Unfortunately, we live in a society in which a man's work is measured by the things which he possesses, where the price of something is of greater importance than its value. Archbishop William Temple used to illustrate this by visualising a window of a shop into which, during the night, some madman had got in and changed all the price tickets. The most valuable things were marked down; the cheap were marked up. This can only too easily happen in our own lives in our acquisitive and affluent society. We are all open to the temptation of devoting our lives to the wrong end; getting, holding, keeping, competing, collecting, till death do us part from them all.

Another false solution to the problem of living with oneself is to abandon the effort to find meaning in life and to allow oneself to drift downstream like a leaf borne by the waters until the inevitable rapids come and, with them, the end, the plunge into nothingness. Some years ago, in somewhat dramatic circumstances, I once encountered someone drifting, just like that. She had never needed, this woman, to earn her own living. The boundaries of her life were the occasional party, gossip with neighbours, a round of golf when she felt like it. She married a man much older than herself and for five years her life was heightened by his presence. Then he died, suddenly, and she was haunted by a sense of loneliness and futility. In her loneliness and futility she began to drink heavily. One evening, with the radio on, she fell into an alcoholic stupor. It lasted until morning. And then, when she woke, the radio was still on and through it came a voice—it happened to be my own—giving a talk on the very subject of making the most of one's life. It chanced that that very morning I was talking about a wasted life and the futility of turning to temporary escape, like drink.

She heard me saying that it was possible to find, through God, in the service of others, an entirely new life. Immediately she sat down and wrote me asking how she could find God as a living reality. I was able to give her a course of action which led, under God, to an answer. In the city where I lived and worked there was a vacancy for the post of assistant matron in a home for old people. She applied. She was appointed. For the next fifteen years she devoted herself to the care of old people. And now she has retired, having found her real self, all those years ago.

Let's look closely at this actual instance of learning to live. That woman did three things: she faced herself, she forgot herself and she died to herself. Here are three basically important principles. Indeed, they are the secret of living, as Christ taught, often. In his story the prodigal, the young man, remember, actually did those three things. He faced himself; he was there among the swine, dirty, disgusting, and in a far country. Secondly, he forgot himself, by remembering his father who, when his son returned home, came more than half-way to meet him, as God will come half-way to meet us. Third, he died to himself in the service of the home that he ought never to have left, the home which is God's home.

And now let's look again at these three basic essentials of a whole life: the necessity to face oneself; the need to remember God our Father; the need, as a response to his love, to go out into the service of others. Facing oneself is never easy. It involves the recognition that we are in a far country, separated from reality by our failure to live as God would have us live; our pride in rags, not necessarily because of what the world considers sins, but more often by sheer forgetfulness of God. Remembering the Father need not be difficult. He is so close to us all the time. He is with us even in the far country of our forgetfulness of him. 'Closer is he than breathing, and nearer than hands or feet.'

We should be willing to go out into the service of others, because the hallmark of the Father's forgiveness is the call to love. We cannot be forgiven and still remain loveless. This call to mission I am trying to make is not, as I have already said, an invitation to escape from the world's challenges. It is exactly the opposite. I am here to remind you that God's forgiveness for our forgetfulness of him must lead to a willingness on our part to take part in loving service, in order that we may love because he first loved us.

So tonight in the presence of Jesus Christ we can look at our lives in an attempt to see them as he sees them, in all their weakness, their inadequacies, their futilities, their dullnesses, their ordinariness, their failures. But none of those things matter. The really important question is not 'am I good?' but; 'am I good for anything?'. That is the first question we need to ask of ourselves.

We have also to give as much as we know of ourselves to as much as we see of Christ—in other words, we have to start where we are, not to wait until we become perfect, which will never, of course, happen. We have to start here and now by giving ourselves, as much as we see of ourselves, to as much as we see of Jesus Christ. We have, too, to be prepared to say: 'Lord, where would you have me go from here: what would you have me to do?' I have no doubt that he will show you. 'In that hour it will be shown you what ye shall do.' It may be that you have got to put right some relationship that has gone wrong. It may be that you must restore to somebody what you have taken. It may be that you must write a letter of apology—by no means always the small thing which it may sound. I do not know what God will tell you to do. But of one thing I am certain: that you will find that he will speak to you and show you in a very practical way where and in what way your life can become different.

Only the Lord can grant us forgiveness and a chance to start again. But if we want it enough, we will find it through him. The most glorious discovery in life is the discovery of our Lord's forgiveness, not just for the things that we have done wrong, but for the things that we have not done right, for missed opportunities, for the missing of the full life of service which we might have lived, but for our cowardices and compromise. Jesus comes to us with the question he put to the man lying by the Pool of Bethesda: 'Will you be made whole?' The man said: 'I have nobody to put me into the water.' Jesus said: 'Get up, take up your bed and walk!' Go out in faith, he is saying to us, into a new and triumphant life of wholeness and usefulness. The man in the story, significantly, was immediately made whole. And this can happen to us, now. On this very first night of this mission, we can go out of this Cathedral into the creative service of our fellow men. Tomorrow will come with all its thrilling opportunities of service. But first, there must be a moment of encounter and that moment is now. We must not postpone it, nor delay it. Jesus stands in front of every one of us today and asks the simple question that he has asked of men all down the centuries. 'Will you be made whole? Are you willing?'

And so now let us be unhurriedly quiet for a while. These moments could be a moment of decisive change and commitment in your life, because, in the silence God may speak, asking us to give him control of our lives, so that we may be ready to go wherever he may send us, ready to do whatever he may ask, ready to become whatever he may ask us to become, ready to welcome him into our lives and bring us forgiveness, healing, light, guidance and power. He wants us to realise for ourselves tonight what he has done for us, and to accept him as our saviour, friend and leader, who can save us from the results of pride and self-will, and to see in him a friend who will be alongside us forever, and who will guide and strengthen us in his service.

If some of you are ready to accept him you might, in the silence, say to yourselves these words: 'Lord, I accept you as my Saviour, Lord and friend. Lord; I open the door on my life to you. Forgive me my failures. Make me what you want me to become.'

NIGHT 2
MR. TOM COYNE

Tom Coyne, well-known as a television performer, especially in the Midlands of England, where he introduces the BBC programme 'Midlands Today', here on this night of the mission appeared to many for the first time in a private and personal capacity. He is a Roman Catholic.

If anyone has come here tonight expecting to hear from me great theological arguments, then I assure them that they are definitely tuned in to the wrong wavelength. I just wouldn't know where to begin. You see, I look on Christianity as a very simple thing. I think that over the years the various denominations have tended to complicate it, and for the layman it gets increasingly difficult to understand some of the theological arguments, the dogma, the weighty pronouncements that are made from time to time.

To me Christianity is a simple thing; a union of love; of understanding; of joy. 'Learn to live with others'— that is our theme tonight. Isn't it sad, that after two thousand years of Christianity, we still have to learn to do that? Something must have gone wrong somewhere. If Christians had learned to live together two thousand years ago, then you, I suppose, would not be Anglicans; I would not be a Roman Catholic; that man over there would not be a Methodist; and your next door neighbour would not be a Salvationist. We were all just plain Christians. . . .

It's often said that a visitor from Mars would find it difficult to understand why there are so many denominations in the Christian Church; why so many people who believe in the same God, why so many people who believe in the same Christ, just cannot get along together. Something must have gone wrong somewhere. A religion based on love has, over the centuries, been involved in so much hate. We have all, at some time or another, had some experience of this. We have all had our own little touches of intolerance. As a boy I always had the feeling that I would be struck down dead if I came inside a Protestant church. I had a sort of deep-rooted feeling that there was something wrong about other denominations, as if all Protestants were heretics, hewing out a pathway for themselves to hell. You might have had the same feelings about the Roman Catholic Church.

Well, as you see, I came in here tonight and the roof hasn't fallen in! I haven't been stoned by the mob! I was invited to come here and I am delighted to speak in a church where I find the same God; the same Christ; and, listening now, more than eight thousand of us where once there were only twelve. Isn't it about time that we now looked on ourselves not as Roman Catholics, or Anglicans, or Baptists, or Methodists; but just as Christians?

To get back to what I was saying a moment ago about the reminders of childhood intolerance. The lads of the Church of England School were the 'Protty Dogs'. I was one of the 'Catty Dogs'. I still have the scars to prove it. Religious wars in the back lanes were daily events. There was no getting on together, no learning to live with the other fellow, trying to understand his point of view. They couldn't understand why we had all this mumbo-jumbo of the Latin in the Mass; why we sprinkled ourselves with holy water. We couldn't understand at all how their clergymen actually got married and had children. In the past few years all of these things, thank God, seem to be undergoing a great change. People, at last, seem to be getting together, to be understanding one another. But we all know that there are still many problems. There are still clergymen who parade with banners when the Pope receives the Archbishop of Canterbury. There are still Roman Catholic priests who believe it wrong that Catholics like myself should be standing here speaking in an Anglican cathedral. Perhaps you and I should get together and let all the priests fight all the battles on the theological front while we, the lay people, show the way by getting together worshipping God, together, as we are all doing here tonight.

What on earth has happened over the last two thousand years of Christianity? Has it had any real influence on the

33

world? We were fighting wars then and we're still fighting them today. . . . This is a Christian country, yet in the past few years, as part of my job on television and radio, I have covered hundreds of stories about our own immigrant problems. . . . I believe that there is no place for intolerance in the Christian make-up. I think that if we can't live together; if we can't love our neighbours; if we can't accept that they have a right to live; that they have a right to be here; that they have a right to enjoy just as good a life, just as high a standard of living as we do ourselves, then we cannot really claim to be a supporter of the founder of our movement.

My grandfather was one of the most devout Roman Catholics I ever knew. He went to Mass every day of his life, and every day of his life he received Holy Communion. But there was one thing he did which taught me more about Christianity than all of that. One of his greatest friends was a little lay preacher for a Free Church, which was in a back street quite near to where we lived. On Sunday afternoons my grandfather used to go out with him and help to put up this portable pulpit which he always had. They used to put it up in a field near a slag heap, and there the preacher used to get up and speak to groups of miners who were playing pitch and toss. You can imagine the sort of reception he used to get! But the fact that my grandfather believed that this man had a right to do that, although he was not a member of his church, made a great impression on me, and it is something—one of these little things in life—that helps to colour one's own approach to things.

All of us here tonight have something to be very grateful and thankful for. We are all Christians; the Christian is never alone; the Christian never needs to seek the comforts of drug addiction. We hear every day of

34

thousands of young people turning to drugs as the answer to their problems. A Christian never needs to do that because he knows there is always someone he can turn to. When I was a kid I would have been described as being a 'Holy Joe' for telling you this now. But why not say it? We all know that there is a God, so let's get up and shout it from the roof-tops. . . . In learning to live with others we are all sharing this joy. Let's remember that one of the most difficult people to live with is yourself, because you are the only human being who knows really what you are thinking. You cannot escape from yourself. Sometimes that little conscience which we all have might be working overtime. We all know it; we all make mistakes; probably at least every day of our lives. We all know, because conscience tells us, that we have slipped up somewhere. But as Christians, all the advantages are on our side. In the words of the once popular song: 'We can all pick ourselves up, we can dust ourselves down, and we can start all over again.' I think that the time has come for us to start all over again: to follow the example which was given two thousand years ago. If God can become man—can learn to live with us—then I shouldn't think it would be too difficult for us to 'learn to live with others'.

MRS. MARGARET GILLESPIE
A PERSONAL STATEMENT

Wife of a pharmaceutical chemist, Margaret Gillespie is an active member of the Cathedral congregation at Coventry.

Nobody really likes a wayward child who is bent on

getting his own way, and throws a tantrum when he doesn't manage it. And yet, how many of us, although according to our age we may be considered adult, are nevertheless wayward and rebellious children as far as God our father is concerned.

For thirty years I was very much a wayward child, living my own life, choosing my friends, my career, my husband, and as far as possible organising things for my pleasure and convenience. I was brought up by very good, very hard-working parents, in what was nevertheless a non-Christian home. And so the Church meant very little to me and the few religious friends that I made used to embarrass me horribly when they talked about God and Jesus and praying, and I used to change the subject to more normal things as quickly as possible.

It often happens, that within a family fear and resentment play an unhappy part in relationships between parents and children, and I am sorry to say that my family was no exception.

And so, at eighteen, determined to be independent, I left my home town, as I thought, for ever. The following years were happy ones—good days at college with a glorious sense of freedom and then starting on my career. True, there was the anxiety of waiting for a fiancé who, during the war years, was almost constantly at sea. But then came marriage, a child, very few material possessions but much happiness and contentment. In fact, life was good; but without God.

Then came a series of crises in swift succession, for which I was quite unprepared. Nervous depression, following the birth of a second child; my father's serious illness; and because of this the need to uproot from our happy little home and our many friends, and return to a place that held such bitter memories for me. Then my father's death was closely followed by that of a very dearly-loved friend. Hatred and resentment, bitterness and frustration, created un unendurable tension which could only be relieved by the taking of tranquileisers, on which I became very dependent. For two and a half years this went on, until the strain of trying to pretend for the sake of the family, drove me to desperation and I knew that I must make a choice—a psychiatrist or a church. The text of the first sermon that I heard was 'The years that the locusts have eaten'. It seemed to have been written just for me, and for the first time I began to see myself as I really was—completely self-centred. Relying on my own strength for a long time had been utterly exhausting, and later on I came to see that God had allowed me to go on my own foolish way and reach this point of despair, in order that I would realise my need of him.

Then began the upward climb: going to Church; confirmation; learning to pray. I was beginning to live again, though not completely. I still relied far too much on what I now call my 'crutches'. They were foolish things, like favourite radio programmes, and the problem pages in women's magazines, and still the sedatives. All these temporarily helped me to forget my own fears and inadequacies.

Looking back on that time in my life I see it as a jigsaw puzzle—the pieces gradually fitting together to make a whole. But we all know how we can spend hours on a jigsaw puzzle and suddenly find that a vital part is missing. I found the missing piece of my Christian life at Lee Abbey, actually, and the missing piece was Jesus Christ. I gave my life to him at a house-party there and, through praying, through getting to know him as a person and a friend, through Bible-reading and through Christian fellowship, I began the experience of God which I so desperately needed. Many people need it today, whether they realise it or not. Christian folk, who sensed my need, prayed for me, and some of the crutches I threw away immediately. Others were taken from me during the following months. In admitting to God my sin of self-concern, and accepting his forgiveness and his very self at the service of holy communion, in seeking his will for my life, his grace began to enter it, cleansing, healing, re-making. To turn from God, and then to other people, away from oneself, living with others, among others, for others, all of which are themes for these mission meetings. Loving people, not just in an emotional way, but wanting the very best for them, is only possible if we, and they, belong to Christ. And this I have found to be true.

The Second Talk
LEARN TO LIVE WITH OTHERS

Last night we were thinking upon a subject which is basic to all personal living; learning to live with yourself. To-night we are looking at a related subject which is basic to the life of the world of today and of tomorrow—learning to live with others. Unless we face up to the questions involved our future is, I think, questionable. Let me read to you a passage from Colin Morris's book *Include Me Out*.[1]

'The other day a Zambian dropped dead only a hundred yards from my front door. The pathologist said he had died from hunger. In his shrunken stomach were a few leaves, and what appeared to be a ball of grass and

[1] Colin Morris, *Include Me Out*. Epworth.

nothing else.' The writer adds: 'The world is not perishing for lack of stronger, better-organised churches; it is perishing for lack of bread.'

That African was one out of those two of every three members of the human race who are not asking for news of the latest venture in Christian unity, or in the restructuring of this or that church. They are asking a much simpler question: 'Where does my next meal come from?' I believe that one trouble with the Church today is that we are concentrating on the wrong things: on matters of internal organisation rather than on external needs. We are talking about changes in the worship of churches when, unless we get our priorities right, there will be no people coming to those churches. We are concentrating on principles rather than on people, on theology rather than sociology, on dialogue with people rather than dynamic confrontation with God. We are busy with the wrong things, in other words, dashing from meeting to meeting, from conference to conference, darting in our minds from one statistic to another and, as regards the things that matter, often getting nowhere at all.

In the last century Benjamin Disraeli told this country that there were two nations: the nation of the haves, and the nation of the have-nots. Much of that inequality has now been erased. But, though there are no longer two nations, there are two worlds. There is the world of the well-fed, and the world of the poor and hungry. While you and I are occupying ourselves with inessentials, millions are starving. It may be that some of those present here tonight came in the expectation that this meeting was going to be concerned only with spiritual matters. But this is not entirely so. We shall be speaking of material matters also; but I would want to make it absolutely plain that there is not now, nor ever has been, a strict division between the two. The sacred is secular and the secular is sacred in many areas of human life, and none more so than in that area which concerns the needs of others. So this matter of learning to live with others is a spiritual issue. And also it should be said that this matter of learning to live with others spells the life or death of a world. It also spells the life and death of our immortal souls, for Jesus said, in that tremendous judgment passage of the twenty-fifth chapter of Matthew: 'I tell you this: anything you did not do for one of these, however humble, you did not do for me.'

I think I should quote the whole of that passage in order to put the sentence I have referred to in its full and memorable context.

'When the Son of Man comes in his glory and all the angels with him, he will sit in state on his throne, with all the nations gathered before him. He will separate men into two groups, as a shepherd separates the sheep from the goats, and he will place the sheep on his right hand and the goats on his left. Then the king will say, to those on his right hand, "You have my father's blessing; come, enter and possess the kingdom that has been ready for you since the world was made. For when I was hungry you gave me food; when thirsty, you gave me drink; when I was a stranger you took me into your home; when naked you clothed me; when I was ill you came to my help; when in prison you visited me." Then the righteous will reply "Lord, when was it that we saw you hungry and fed you, or thirsty and gave you drink, a stranger and took you home, or naked and clothed you?" And the king will answer "I tell you this: anything you did for one of my brothers here, however humble, you did for me." Then he will say to those on his left hand: "The curse is upon you; go from my sight to the eternal fire that is ready for the devil and his angels. For while I was hungry you gave me nothing to eat, when thirsty nothing to drink; when I was a stranger you gave me no home, when naked you did not clothe me; when I was ill and in prison you did not come to my help." And they too will reply, "Lord, when was it that we saw you hungry or thirsty, or a stranger or naked or ill or in prison, and did nothing for you?" And he will answer: "I tell you this; anything you did not do for one of these, however humble, you did not do for me." '

This is a highly relevant passage, speaking to the condition of all of us today. Sometimes as I sit in my study I see before me, in my mind's eye, the faces of hungry children; I see bodies burnt by napalm; I see thousands of refugees. These are not distant generalities. They are matters of pressing concern. But before we can hope to respond to their challenge; to place ourselves in the right frame of mind from which alone we can exercise practical compassion to the needy at a distance, it is essential that we examine critically the quality of our personal relationships in our daily lives. We must get these right before we can even begin on the more distant, less personal concern for others to which the state of the world calls us.

It is a searching exercise, to ask ourselves in a moment of quiet thought, whether there is anyone we despise. It is a searching question to ask ourselves whether there are people from whom we are held off by reason of their habits, their opinions, or even perhaps their colour? We must ask ourselves whether we can be sure that there are no people, moreover, whom we have failed to help, in the distant past, in the recent past, even in the last few days or weeks. We must ask ourselves who we have passed by on the other side. On the day of judgment, let it be remembered, we shall not be judged by our sins of commission;

but by our sins of omission. We shall be judged by the things that we have not done while yet there was time for them to be done; by the people we never loved or helped, while yet there was the opportunity. I doubt very much whether any of us can survive unfaulted such self-examination. We are all sinners in this respect before God—that we have failed to love completely what the Bible has called the brethren; the people we work with, the members of our family, our neighbours, all, in fact, with whom life brings us into close contact.

What did Jesus have to say about these personal relationships? He talked about forgiveness, he talked about love; he talked about service; he talked about acceptance. Forgiveness, to take the first, can be dynamic in action. Years ago I knew a couple who, as it happened, lived in Hong Kong. They had been married for many years. For the first ten, their marriage was very happy. Then it gradually deteriorated, the process of disintegration starting with jealousy, then suspicion, then coldness, interspersed by occasional periods of active dislike. Towards the end, when all seemed lost, the wife decided to come home for a period. Here, as it happened or, as I would prefer to say, as God willed it, she came into a profound experience of the love and forgiveness of Jesus Christ; her eyes were opened to the love of Christ and she realised in the light of it one tremendous thing—that, despite everything, Jesus still loved her. It sounds a very simple thing. But it changed her life. Immediately she wanted to go back as soon as possible and to put it right with her husband, and to go out and tell everybody about it. She went back. As the ship was docking she looked down from the deck and saw a crowd of people standing there underneath. Her eye lighted on a handsome, middle-aged man. With a shock of surprise she realised it was her husband whom she was seeing with new eyes. Within a matter of hours she had begun to tell him where she had been wrong, and this led him, in his turn, to confess his part in what was causing the break-up in their marriage. When I met them many years later, not long before they died, they said that life began again when they found the wonder of forgiveness and rebirth.

So the first truth Jesus tells us about concerning this matter of living with others is the need for forgiveness from God and for one another, followed by an offering of love. How much this matters, how important it is we can sometimes see, by noting what happens when such opportunities are missed.

Here is an actual instance. A friend of mine, as it happens a clergyman, got in touch some years ago with one of life's drop-outs—a man who had failed, very obviously, in most things in life which he had touched. He was useless; he felt despised and rejected by the world. He had many serious personality deficiencies and, to add to all, he was virtually an alcoholic. But in this friend of mine he thought that he had found a friend. At first, at any rate, this was true, because my friend was prepared to listen and to give him time. This proved more demanding than he had bargained for. The man whom he had befriended came often to see him. Indeed, he came often and often, until his presence became burdensome. My friend came to feel that his own time was being too much consumed by this one person and so, becoming more and more impatient, one day when the man called my friend left a message that he was out. It was the one day when he should have been loving and welcoming and considerate, because the man went home, turned on the gas, closed the windows, and died. It need never have happened if there had not been a failure in patience and in love.

True, we cannot love everybody. But God can, through us. Love expressed in personal service is of the utmost importance. Let me give you an actual instance of that.

Some months ago, when a group of lay people in this diocese were gathered together in the vicar's study, thinking and talking about their responsibilities towards the world, the vicar's wife came in and told them that she had been looking at a television programme about orphans from Vietnam. Suddenly, the whole group became aware that their responsibilities might start there, in that very place with that very issue. They began to ask what they could do, and soon discovered that they could do something. Firstly they raised a sum of money, and they began to read and to pray about the problem. Then they advertised for two Christian nurses, and they found them. Then the vicar went out to Vietnam to prepare the way for the two nurses to go there also. And now, at this moment, they are hard at work in that distant land, looking after homeless children. Only a few days ago one child whose father and mother were killed was allowed to leave the country and has now been taken over in this island by a British family.

What an achievement! One baby in the eyes of God is an immortal soul. It reminds me of the Good Samaritan story, of the man who fell among thieves and was left lying in the dust by the side of the road as two outwardly good people passed him by. They were good; but they were just not good enough. Then a stranger walked across. He became involved, this Samaritan, gave care and help. And this is precisely what Jesus did and does. He does not wait until we are good enough. He does not wait until we are morally respectable. He comes when we are in need and he offers us his service and when we know of our need, we acknowledge it.

The greatest power in the world is the power to open a human heart by acceptance, and that power comes from Jesus who for thirty years was identified with us and accepted us as we are. This is a strong fact for any to hold on to, who feel, as some do, that they are beyond acceptance. Let them think again. The great question that everyone of us has to answer is this: are we prepared to accept Christ's acceptance? The one thing that usually prevents us from doing so is pride. We want to earn forgiveness, and we cannot do it. Many people have found disillusionment upon this road. But Jesus loves us and welcomes us as we are, which is a tremendously releasing and relieving truth. The prodigal son smelled of the pigsty, when his father, on his return, wrapped his mantle around him. And so the secret of effectively living together is to respond to the initiative of God's love. Gratitude comes when we do; gratitude issuing in responsible, self-giving love.

Only this afternoon I was writing a letter to a priest who had failed tragically. I said: 'The one thing you must not do is to wallow. If you remain covered with self-pity then you remain lost forever. You have fallen; accept the Lord's forgiveness and rise. You will have more to give now than you have ever had to give before, because you have found forgiveness and you will be filled with gratitude.'

Let me end with two questions. Do we still really believe that we can work our way into the kingdom of God by our own self-effort? If we think so we are wrong. Secondly, do we really believe that the love of God is undemanding? If we think that, we are wrong again. God must find it very difficult to get on with you and me. He must find it very difficult very often. But he has accepted us and so we can accept others in his strength. And now here is the great truth which brings us back to our starting point— the problem of living with others in a world of conflict.

It is this; it is out of the multiplication of countless personal acts of reconciliation that a new world can be built, and it is again out of this multiplication of personal acts of reconciliation that the tensions of domestic, social, racial, industrial and political animosities can and will be resolved.

There is no other way. It is the way of the cross, the way of humiliation, the way of acceptance, the way of involvement, the way laid down by Jesus, who left the throne of glory and came to be alongside us. The real test as to whether we can follow the way of the Cross lies in how much we really care, how much we really love. And the way to care and to love is to discover we are loved so that, in return and in response, we begin to allow ourselves to become involved, to let ourselves go in compassion, to love others in the strength of him who first loved us. There is a prayer which I sometimes use and which I would like to commend to you: 'Lord, help me to accept your love, to be filled with your love, and with it to begin to love those who up to now I have not loved. Help me to forgive, and make me willing to be forgiven. Lord, take me, just as I am, and make me what you would have me to be.'

* * *

NIGHT 3
MR. LEWIS DAVEY

L. J. Davey, formerly an accountant, joined the staff of the Bishop of Coventry as Bishop's Personal Assistant more than a decade ago. He spoke on this occasion, however, in a personal capacity on a personal matter.

We live in an uncertain world. None of us know what will happen tomorrow, so today we try to build for ourselves as much security as possible. But fears continue to hold us. For much of the time we keep them at bay; but we can never really forget them: not just fears of war or natural disasters, but personal fears: fear of death, fear of bereavement, fear of ill-health, fear of our inability to cope, especially if called upon to bear pain. This fear of the unknown future, though common to us all, gives us a sense of being alone. We try not to think about it, for if we do we feel lost, like being in an unknown country without guide, signposts, compass or maps. But some of us have been in that unknown country and have come back with good news. There *is* a guide, and there *is* a way through. Many of you know this, but others do not, and to help them I want to tell my own experience. I do so with some diffidence, for what I shall say I have spoken of to only one or two people, but it is no use theorising about sufferings. The only thing that helps in the long run is the sympathy born of personal experience.

After the last war, my wife and I left London to live in the peace and beauty of the countryside. We were very happy there. The lovely Downs and the sea only five miles away made my daily journey to the City a very small price to pay. The war was over, we had a good income, a comfortable home, good health, many friends. Life was good. Then, out of a clear sky, disaster struck.

The doctor was called in to see my wife for what seemed to be a minor ailment, and advised an immediate operation. Our worst fears were realised. The most we could hope for was that the disease had been checked. For three years we lived with our fears, sustained and upheld by our Christian faith, which, incidentally, I had rejected for the first thirty years of my life. And then, the agony of frustrated and disappointed hope came. Another operation and another time of waiting and learning to live a day at a time was upon us. But the day came, five years after the first blow had struck us, when it became clear that medical science could do no more.

Then began the nightmare which many have experienced. How would we react when physical pain became intolerable? Could she bear the suffering? Could I bear to see her suffer? And in all this where was God? What had our faith in Christ to give us now? Was it, after all, something we had clung to just to make life bearable; but quite impotent in the face of the real, daily, actual stress of mind and spirit to which we were now subjected?

We had prayed and prayed, with what result? Perhaps, I thought, my earlier agnosticism had been more realistic.

One day I went into a church to pray. In agony of mind I battered the gates of heaven for my wife's recovery. Suddenly, it was as if a restraining hand was laid upon me, and as though a voice said 'Stop!' 'Pray only that God's will be done, and all will be well. Be still and leave everything to him.' In a moment of time I felt the whole burden fall from my shoulders. I knew what Job meant when he cried 'I know that my redeemer liveth'. Two days later my wife and I went to a service of healing conducted by a man who had been struck blind many years before and had endured very great sufferings. Within a week my wife's condition showed a remarkable improvement. Colour returned to her cheeks, appetite came back and by the end of a month she was walking over the downs. She even put on weight, which is almost unknown for one suffering from her particular illness. But, far more important than all this was the complete relief from anxiety and fear. The next four months were a time of very real happiness. Everything we did had a heightened joy; the plays we saw, the books we read, the music we heard. No longer did we doubt God's love and care for us. We did not ask about the future. We were content to live a day at a time. We were no longer lost in a dark indifferent world. God was with us, and we knew we could trust him.

Then, one day, she did not awake from sleep, except for a brief moment of clarity when she spoke a few words of peace and joy. She was healed and she was safe.

That was fourteen years ago, almost to the day, but the memory of those days of suffering are as vivid as if they were only yesterday, and remembering the way in which God revealed himself to us in all his power and love, I am saddened by the blind ignorance of the humanist and those who can conceive of God as no more than an impersonal force or, worse still, as an invention of man to make life bearable. None of us can escape suffering and few, if any, can solve its mysteries. There may be some great souls who can bear it with stoicism and fortitude; but they are the exceptions. We need a helper, and it is Jesus Christ who comes to us in our sickness, and so transforms our sufferings that our lives are enriched.

I end by quoting some words that my wife spoke to me before her death. She said: 'I know now that no matter what we have to bear, or where we have to go, Christ is there, and has borne it for us, and we having nothing to fear.'

MRS. DAVIS
A PERSONAL STATEMENT

Mrs. Davis was a widow who, after a bereavement, lost the sight of both eyes; but has nonetheless steadily grown since then in the experience of God's love. She was interviewed by Canon Geoffrey Rogers and, because of the special nature of her narrative and situation, the interview is given here in full.

ROGERS: Mrs. Davis, we are thinking tonight about 'Learning to live with suffering' and of the wonderful way God can carry those who trust him through the most tragic troubles in life. Suffering has come to you through bereavement and now, more recently, blindness. And yet you did not always feel sure, as you do now. Is this something which you have been learning over the years?

MRS. DAVIS: This is something which has come slowly through the years; but it has been worth waiting for.

ROGERS: When you were quite young, had you a clear faith and trust in God as you have now?

MRS. DAVIS: No, I had a yearning to find out, and to find out what it was all about; but it was not very steadfast in those days.

ROGERS: Then you grew up and you were very happily married, in 1932. Did your husband share your faith?

MRS. DAVIS: He did not attend the Church. I don't know why: he was a very good living man and I do believe that he had a faith. But there was something lacking in his faith, as there was in mine at that time.

ROGERS: And so together you were both learning more, and during the war you seemed to learn more quickly. Why was that?

MRS. DAVIS: Well, I had living with me at that time a young girl, an evacuee from Coventry, and I felt it was my duty as an older person to see that this child was taken regularly to church, and this I did, going with her, because the example had to be set to a younger person.

ROGERS: And then your husband became ill. What effect did you find that had on you?

MRS. DAVIS: This had a very strong effect on us. He was ill for over twenty years, mentally, and very seriously physically ill. We prayed that he might get better and, having no answer, we prayed that he might die to relieve him of the terrible suffering he was in. But we had to learn that this was not the way to pray. We prayed then for strength to get through each day as it came, and this way we found that we were able to live with the suffering. In 1962 he died. Death came as a very welcome visitor to us. We had longed that he should be relieved of pain, and this was not possible in mortal life, and I believe that death was the beginning of the true life that he had to live—release from all the pain that he had on this earth.

ROGERS: Did this in any way lessen your own faith in God?

MRS. DAVIS: No: I think in fact it strengthened it because what we had longed for so long had at last come about, and I started immediately to attend Church regularly and to try and find out more and more about Christ and about his teaching. Three years ago I lost the sight of one eye. My first reaction to this was that I had had enough. I thought through all the years that we had had of pain and suffering, that I at least deserved a little bit of a better chance, and I felt that this was the finish. If I couldn't even see, I'd be done with it. Then the words came into my mind 'Cast thy burden on the Lord' and I didn't go into any prayer for this, I just said 'Right; you can have the worry. I have finished with it.' And I had.

ROGERS: Yet only four months ago you lost the sight of the other eye. Wasn't that absolutely the end?

MRS. DAVIS: No. This is the beginning. It was a wonderful experience. I had been feeling very depressed and down and all at once I was enveloped in loving kindness. The warmth of it was physically felt. It was true, and sight didn't matter any more. Suddenly I was conscious of kindness and loving thought around me, which has wrapped round me ever since, and sometimes I think I must look too happy, really, because you can't keep it back—it's bubbling up all the time. It's been a wonderful experience.

The Third Talk
LEARN TO LIVE WITH SUFFERING

We are going to think together tonight about learning to live with suffering. Sooner or later every one of us is going to have to experience it, in greater or lesser degree. The Christian faith is not an insurance policy against suffering. How can it be when Christ himself suffered grievously, and was himself a man of sorrows and acquainted with grief? So suffering is bound to come, and it is important that we should learn to be prepared for it when it does.

So we are not concerned now about how to get rid of suffering, which in any event is impossible; but with how to live with suffering, and it is important not to underestimate the gravity or the grimness of the matter. Those of us who have suffered very little must beware of speaking or thinking of this in facile terms. There is nothing easy about suffering. There is nothing dignified about suffering. And yet—strange to say—whenever I, for one, am depressed, I go to a Home, near here, which is devoted to the care of incurables. Many are almost totally immobilised: most know pain and acute discomfort as constant daily conditions and have no expectation of anything else while life lasts. And yet—and here is a mystery at the heart of suffering—I came away from that place as though I had received a tonic. For there I have encountered victorious living. That home for incurables is, in an extraordinary manner, an antidote to depression.

It is necessary to ponder on this mystery. It is necessary to reflect on the strange fact that this suffering has at the core of it the possibility of being creative and ennobling. I think of two examples both associated with this Cathedral. I think of Richard Dimbleby, who at the time of the consecration in 1962 was the chief television commentator. At that time the world did not know what he knew, that he had only a few years to live. Yet through his courage, through the dignity with which he faced, and lived, the time he had left, he became an inspiration to millions. I think of Sir Malcolm Sargent. He might have been here with us tonight, for he had promised to conduct the music of this mission. Just before his death I had a letter from him telling me that the doctors had said he had, at the most, six weeks to live. He lived six days. Throughout those days I am told that he was able to maintain his marvellous debonair courage, through the transforming power of the Christ whom he had loved and sought to serve throughout the previous years.

Of course, it would be utterly wrong to imply that only Christians can suffer creatively. Some non-Christians have set marvellous examples. Nevertheless we can learn much from entering into the sufferings of Christ, who taught us how to go through suffering not only creatively, but redemptively.

There are five basically important truths to be learned from a study of our Lord's sufferings. First, his life was one of identification, leading to deep compassion. On the cross and through the cross Christ drew more people to himself than at any other period of his life. He converted a Roman centurion, a man of Cyrene, Joseph of Arimathea, some women of Jerusalem, and a robber dying alongside him. And then there is the matter of acceptance: the Lord did not fight against suffering: rather he found in and through it creative peace. There are some memorable words of Henry Drummond's, written years ago, about this, words quoted by Evelyn Underhill in her book *The Fruits of the Spirit*:

'Christ's life, outwardly, was one of the most troubled lives that was ever lived. Tempest and tumult, tumult and tempest, waves breaking over it all the time, but the inner life was a sea of glass, the great calm was always there. At any moment you might have gone to him and found rest, even when the bloodhounds were dogging him in the streets of Jerusalem he turned to his disciples and offered them as a last legacy, peace. Peace, in the middle of it all; what an extraordinary and wonderful gift! "Peace I leave to you. My peace I give unto you." '

The third truth we can learn from Christ's suffering is co-operation with the divine and loving plan. The crucifixion is not the story of a pliant victim being dragged to his death. It is the story of the creative, loving, overruling plan of a divine and loving father. Christ realised this. He never sought an explanation. He never sought any answers to the question as to why it had to happen to him. But he did say: 'Not my will, but thine be done.' Here was a co-operation with one who rules and overrules. Again

54

Heralding the Coventry Mission

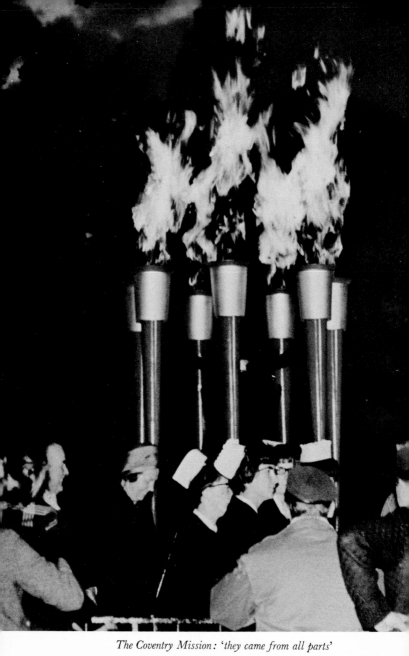

The Coventry Mission: 'they came from all parts'

The Bishop passes through the crowd at the open air Eucharist

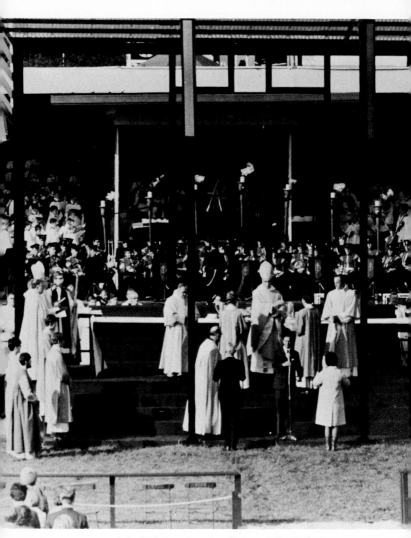

The Bishop receives the offerings at the Eucharist

and again I think of that last word. God overrules the tyranny and sinfulness of man.

Again, through all his sufferings, Christ never ceased to be concerned for others. The traditional words from the cross reflect the fact. 'Father, forgive them', 'Woman, behold your son', 'Today you will be with me in paradise.' Out of the world full of suffering these unforgettable prayers emerge. And then—perhaps the strangest truth of all, there was the joy that filled his heart. Recall the words of scripture: 'Who for the joy that was set before him endured the cross.' Christ never lost sight of ultimate victory, and that is what enabled him to be filled with joy.

But, is not this approach, as some critics would maintain, too lugubrious, implying that it is man only in his weakness who can find Christ? I do not think so. Suffering is an inescapable part of the human condition. Self-sufficient man is rather terrifying. St. Paul, as usual, has something striking to say about this. He wrote to the Corinthians: 'Make no mistake about this, if there is anyone among you who fancies himself wise, wise I mean by the standards of this passing age, he must become a fool to gain true wisdom, for the wisdom of this world is folly in God's sight.'

To men and women in their weakness Jesus Christ has most movingly and fruitfully spoken, because often we must experience the need for him before we discover him. It is from our needs that we go to our knees. Men and women riding high in their success have no needs. That is what makes it so hard for self-sufficient people, whose eyes are not open to the sufferings of people around them, or to their own real needs, to see the Christ at all. It is in times of sorrow and dereliction that we hear a still small voice, perhaps the voice of the psalmist: 'Out of the depths have I called unto thee, O Lord.' Or we may hear Christ's own words: 'Come unto me all whose work is hard and whose load is heavy and I will give you strength.'

Let us go out from this place and look around to the lonely and the aged and the emotionally disturbed. Let us go out from this place and try to get alongside them. If we do so we shall find that Christ is there, among the suffering. Here is a wonderful prayer by the Abbé Quoist: 'Lord, why did you tell me to love all men—my brothers? I tried, but I come back to you frightened . . . Lord, I was so peaceful at home, I was so comfortably settled. It was well furnished, and I felt cozy. I was alone, I was at peace. . . . As soon as I started to open the door I saw them, with outstretched hands, burning eyes, longing hearts, like beggars on church steps. The first ones came in, Lord. There was after all some space in my heart. I welcomed them. I would have cared for them and fondled them, my very own little lambs, my little flock. You would have been pleased, Lord, I would have served and honoured you in a proper, respectable way. But the next ones, Lord, the other men, I had not seen them; they were hidden behind the first ones. We had to crowd in, I had to find room for them. Now they have come from all over pushing one another, jostling one another. Lord, they hurt me! they are everywhere. They are in the way. Lord! my door is wide open! I can't stand it any more. It's too much! It's no kind of a life! What about my job? my family? my peace? my liberty? Lord, I have lost everything. I don't belong to myself any longer; There's no more room for me at home.'[1]

Don't worry God says, you have gained all. While men came in to you I, your Father, I, your God, slipped in among them.

[1] Michel Quoist, *Prayers of Life*. Gill and Macmillan.

I have left to the last one of the most terrible forms of suffering, a form of it with which this world abounds. And that is suffering caused by hunger and starvation. I quoted last night from a book by Colin Morris, *Include Me Out*. Now I quote again from the same source:

'We are an integrate part of a gluttonous church, in a gluttonous society, the small, white, largely Christian minority are rich and growing richer every day. They're not even twenty per cent of the world, and yet they consume seventy-five per cent of the world income.'

It will not suffice, on the day of judgment, to say: 'Lord, I didn't realise, I didn't understand.' Conversion to Christ is conversion to the world's suffering. Acceptance of Christ means acceptance of Christ's mission to a world in torment. It means going across the road out of isolationism and security to the place where the suffering peoples of the world are to be found. It means taking off our coats, rolling up our sleeves, pulling out our money, being ready for hard work, hard thinking, hard giving of time, talents, money. Jesus stands over there on the other side of the road, among the suffering. We must be willing to go across; if we are, we shall find him there. He is waiting for our help. He is waiting for it now. He wants the remaining years of our lives. Until we have given our lives to him unreservedly, to be used by him in the service of suffering humanity, we cannot claim to be his.

As we look out at this world, human answers to its problems are not enough. Force is no answer. Cleverness is no answer. Power structures are no answer. Christ knew that underneath all suffering, like the bottom of an iceberg, is evil. Christ met this evil with love, and love triumphant in the resurrection is the proof of it. We follow the royal son of God, who calls us out from our comfort. He calls us out from our ordinariness into the extraordinary battle of war against evil. But first we must be very sure that we are his and that we have committed ourselves to him, that we have accepted him. He accepted us in our baptism; have we accepted him in our conversion? That is the question. Have we placed ourselves unreservedly at his disposal? Are we on the Lord's side? The challenge tonight, and every night, is to accept Christ as Saviour and Lord, and to join him in his battle against evil and suffering.

* * *

NIGHT 4
THE REVEREND
DOCTOR LESLIE DAVISON

Leslie Davison is a distinguished Methodist. General Secretary of the Home Mission Department, he was formerly Chairman of the Birmingham and Wolverhampton District of the Methodist Church. On this fourth evening of the mission, he was interviewed by Tom Coyne before the Bishop spoke about Learning to Live through Death. In this account of the interview, the interviewer's questions are omitted, except where they are given in indirect speech, but the gist of Dr. Davison's answers is given.

Having been asked whether he felt that there was anything sad about death, Dr. Davison replied: 'Fundamentally a Christian can face the fact of death, take it courageously and find in it a great and wonderful triumph over his own disappointment and failures and over all the sadness and misery that death itself involves.' He added,

'I think there are two stages in our understanding of death. When people have reached a maturity of life, when their physical and mental powers begin to decay, the idea of death loses all its grimness, and can become something quite welcoming. People feel they don't want to be a burden to themselves or to their loved ones, and many a time I have heard old folks say: "I am just waiting for the Lord to take me." Death to this age group is nothing like the problem it is when it hits in the middle years, in early youth, or when someone is just at the very height of their powers and potentialities. If death hits then, it seems so absurd; there is no rhyme, no reason for it. And if death hits at that time with disfiguring disease, with all the loathsome accompaniment of decay, then something inside one rises up and says: "This is obscene: life is not meant to be lived this way", and the whole futility of death hanging over the human race as a great nightmare is a question that has to be faced.

It would be a sad thing if this life were the only life that man could live. Who would say goodbye to this without something of sadness? But if there is an alternative life, if there is a new development, then this life becomes simply the primary school, and one can be a little impatient if that lasts too long, and be anxious to begin the next stage of the journey.'

Dr. Davison was then asked whether it was not a cruelty in God to leave families without a father or a mother, when death seemed to strike arbitrarily. He replied: 'I think this is where the real fact of death hits home, where we have to answer the profound question: if God is a loving God, and in control of his universe, why does he allow this to happen? And I think you are then forced to the two alternatives: either there is no life after death, in which case the whole human story is an idiocy without rhyme or reason; it began in nothing and it will end in nothing. Or there is the great Christian hope that life goes on. . . . An affluent society today has enabled us to push death away from the centre of living that once it occupied. A hundred and fifty years ago there was a constant procession to the grave. Thousands of children died every year. One could not escape the fact of death. But today it is all done so discreetly that death is hidden away from us so that we scarcely notice its happening . . . —until it does. . . .

I lost my wife about five and a half years ago. Her illness was sudden. Within six or seven months, from being a lovely youthful person, full of life and hope, she was smitten and brutally mauled by disease. She passed after almost indescribable agony. In her passing there was no joy, there was no relief, there was no vision, there was no voice from heaven to comfort. One had to live with the whole dreadful experience. And in the utter darkness, nothing was left except faith. And in time that faith held. One realised that the God who had loved us, who had given us each to the other, was a God who would not let us down. And although we could see no reason in this, although we could not make any sense at all, gradually there was the conviction that that dear life had not been blotted out; that it lived on wherever God was, and as his great love enshrouded us, so she, embodied in that love, still continued as herself. Out of this came the deeper assurance of life beyond and of continuing partnership. About six months after my wife died I had a spectacular dream. I dreamt that I was in a great station concourse, and from the crowd my wife came running towards me. We just held each other for a glorious minute, and then she said: "I know you've got this train to catch. My train goes from Platform 12. It goes out before yours but when we get up the line your train joins on to mine. Come along and find me." When I woke up in the morning I had that wonderful assurance that she was just a stage ahead of me on the journey, and that one day I would go along the corridor and find her. . . .'

SISTER PEGGY BOYNES
A PERSONAL STATEMENT

Peggy Boynes, a Church Army sister, experienced in hostel work and youth work, was seconded to the diocese of Coventry in 1968. She was a member of the executive team of the Call to Mission, and is now working on the follow-up.

I believe in the resurrection of the body and the life of the world to come, and I believe that not just because I've been taught to say it in Church, or because it seems reasonable, or just because I want to believe it. I believe it and I know it to be true—it's so important. I believe in the resurrection of the body and the life of the world to come. I believe it because Jesus Christ has promised life—real life—and certainly in my limited experience as a Christian I find something of this real life, and I believe it because, in his gracious love he has shown me signs and evidence of the life of the world to come.

For a few years before I came to Coventry I had the very real joy and privilege of working in some old people's homes. Our home was not large. There were just twenty elderly ladies and ourselves and the cat, and that was our family. Some of the elderly women had no family, and some were unwanted by their families. But this was our home—a home with a small 'h'.

We all took our part in the daily duties of our home, and the ladies had their small jobs to do; they set the table, they helped with the washing-up; not because they had to, but because they wanted to—because that was their home. They came to live there and they came to die there.

I want to tell you about one of our ladies. She was ninety-two and one day she collapsed. It was just before Christmas. We called the doctor and he told us that she was nearing the end of her earthly life and we must put her to bed. She was a grand Christian soul, who loved the Lord Jesus and had so much to teach us younger folk. Even when we put her to bed we prayed with her because she wanted it this way. We looked after her during the day and in the night. And each night in turn we would draw close while she blessed us. I suppose that isn't very proper in the Church of England; but it seemed sense then. And we prayed together; she talked to God and she talked to us—a sort of triangle. And she watched us, as she lay in her bed, decorate her room for Christmas, and it suddenly struck her that she might not be around for Christmastime, so of course she had to have her Christmas early.

That year we had two Christmases, for we celebrated on the fifteenth—'just in case' she said—for she didn't really want to miss it. But she did live over Christmas and she lived for two months after, and day by day she got very weak and she suffered a great deal.

But each night, even though she was beginning to lose control of her mind, she still turned to her friend, the lord Jesus Christ, and together we would share together.

Does this sound sentimental? I don't really care about

that because this is just what happened. And then, of course, the day came. It was just shortly after this three-cornered conversation: her, myself, and God, that she actually died. It was natural and wholesome. We missed her, because we'd looked after her, and sometimes we had one or two pangs. We would get her tray ready and suddenly realise that it would not be needed. But she was with her friend. It was perfectly natural. And I look to that saint of God, and I want to follow into her footsteps and know my friend, Jesus Christ, so well in this life today, that it will be a very natural thing as I come to know him in the life to come. And I believe in the resurrection of the body and the life of the world to come.

The Fourth Talk
LEARN TO LIVE THROUGH DEATH

Death is the one experience through which every one of us, sooner or later, must pass. Therefore it is realistic that you should begin to look at it before that moment comes. The one thing that is absolutely certain is that, in a hundred years from now, not one of us will be here. But the idea that we shall be *somewhere* has been in people's minds almost as a natural instinct, or as a universal assumption, for thousands of years.

Sometime ago I had the great privilege of being one of the first people to go into the Egyptian King Tutanka-men's tomb not long after it was opened to the public. It was an experience I shall never forget. In that place which had been locked and sealed for thousands of years there lay two bodies: a young king and his still younger wife.

On the forehead of the girl was a sprig of something like rosemary, placed there by the sorrowing husband. All around was silver and gold and weapons. They believed, you see, that there was an after life in which such things would be needed. So those people believed in survival, but there is a sharp distinction between this and the Christian hope. The Christian hope is of the resurrection of the human personality. Obviously, physical life as we know it has an end. The Bible makes it very clear that death is a supreme fact, and that when the body dies it is indeed dead. The Prayer Book is equally clear: 'Ashes to ashes, dust to dust—' are the immemorial words which have been said over many a body as it is committed to the ground. It is important that we should strip death of sentimentality, as well as of the false ideas which have gathered round it. It is not true, for instance, that death is a calamity, unless it comes tragically and early. That is unnatural death. But natural death can be a mercy—and indeed is so often and often. Swift, in one of his lesser known Gulliver's Travels made the point memorably when he wrote about a people called Struldbugs, who were born with a curious mark on their foreheads. The mark indicated that they could not die, and when it was noted there was great lamentation as to the fate which awaited them. They got older and older, and increasingly lonely. Finally, they were objects of pity and so remained, for ever. What a parable is there! Death is merciful when it comes in the fullness of time. St. Francis knew that, describing the means of our final release as Sister Death, to be welcomed like other elemental things, like the stars, like fire, like day and night.

It is mistaken, also, to approach death with resentment, as that which sunders us from material possessions and all the trappings of this life. But, such is our human condition, this is inevitable. 'Naked we came into the world, naked we shall leave it.' Unless we are prepared for that, we shall become increasingly resentful as death approaches in the fullness of time. This is the very opposite of growing old gracefully. The poet James Shirley sums up this matter of the universality of death:

> The glories of our blood and state
> Are shadows, not substantial things,
> There is no armour against fate,
> Death lays his icy hand on kings.
> Sceptre and crown must tumble down
> And in the dust be equal made
> With the poor crooked scythe and spade.

How then should we adjust ourselves to this supreme adventure of death? How prepare for it? First, I think, by facing it and living each day as though it might be our last, and by being ready to go and pack for the journey. Then, and most important of all, we must prepare for it by entering into eternal life now, so that when the death of the body comes, it will be a small thing in a greater whole. In essence we must accept from Jesus now what is his to give—the gift of eternal life, remembering that eternal life is not a going on of life as we know it; but a going into a new life in Christ. I illustrate this for myself by thinking of two people sitting next to each other in an auditorium where a great orchestra is playing. One, very musical, has passed through the music into another world of aesthetic appreciation. But the other, not at all musical, is only conscious of his immediate surroundings. Each is only one yard away from the other; yet the two are in different worlds. Thus it is with eternal life—that gift from Christ which takes us into a heightened awareness of life, and makes all things new.

The actual moment of death, I may add, may not be as

fearful as we sometimes think. We do wrong, and have done much wrong, to surround it with fear and gloom. We must remember that Christ will be with us. His own words at the moment of death were: 'Father, to thy hands I commend my spirit.'

But how are we to adjust not only to the idea of death for ourselves, but to bereavement—the loss of dear ones? We must not be caught unprepared. A newly widowed woman said to a friend of mine: 'My whole life is in ruins: the death of my husband has come as such a shock.' But why a shock? It would not have been so had she been prepared. We know that there comes a moment when this will happen. The great thing is to be ready with faith and hope when it does.

By contrast I think of another widow. As soon as I heard that her husband had died I telephoned her. She had just entered the house from the hospital where he had died. She started straight off: 'I am afraid you must be feeling rather fearful of phoning me at this particular moment. But I can assure you that you needn't worry. My husband went forward with quiet faith. We had some wonderful hours together as we prepared for his journey. And though I shall miss him greatly I am completely confident about the future and I am at peace.' I put the phone down. It was not I who had comforted; it was I who had been comforted.

But death may not come in the fullness of time. Sometimes it strikes at a very early age. I think of a great friend of mine whose little boy died at thirteen. This is what he wrote to me: 'Thank you so much for your letter. My wife and I know that God loaned us Johnny for thirteen years. We did our best to train him for immortality, and now we've handed him back to the Lord who lent him to us.'

And so I come to the main matter of all. What is the

66

Christian hope? It is to be found in three things. First, in the fact of the resurrection. Secondly in the necessity for judgment, and thirdly, in the need for our personal acceptance of Jesus Christ as Lord and Saviour.

As to the resurrection, I have just finished a remarkable book by Michael Green called *Man Alive* in which he writes: 'The resurrection showed Paul that so far from wrestling under God's curse, Jesus was in fact the key to all God's blessing. No wonder Paul went round the ancient world passing on this shattering discovery, of a god who cared enough to stand in for us in the face of our greatest needs. No wonder he insisted on preaching Jesus and the resurrection. In common with the rest of the Christians, he had come into a new dimension of life. He couldn't keep quiet about it—he had to pass it on. For this Jesus who died on the cross and rose three days later held the key to what life was meant to be and what it could be. Here was someone so fully alive that death could not hold him. This was news.'[1]

Yes, the centre of our Christian hope is in the fact of the resurrection, a fact amply proven, witnessed to by millions through the centuries, who have known that their redeemer lives.

The second great reality for Christians is the inevitability of judgment. We shall all be judged because we are all being judged. In a sense, we are judging ourselves, by which I mean that an unwisely lived life brings its own consequences, as many in this age of stress learn unmistakably for themselves. We are judging ourselves all the time. But also—and far more importantly—Christ is judging us: by our love or by our lack of love. Do we really care, do we feel, do we notice, do we pause and give time for people in need? Or are we too turned in

[1] Inter-Varsity Press.

upon ourselves? Do we cross the road to where the needy are, or not? It is precisely because of this inescapable fact of divine judgment that the necessity of decisive acceptance of Jesus Christ as Lord and Saviour cannot be delayed or postponed. It must be faced here and now. The offer of eternal life is now, because the offer of eternal love is now. Eternity begins here and now; we do not slip into the kingdom of God. The Christian life depends upon a solemn contract—God made his part of it when we were baptised. In his love he welcomed us, he washed us, he blessed us, he accepted us. But have we ever accepted him? An act of will is required on our part also: an act of commitment. Eternal life begins with the decisive acceptance of Jesus Christ as Lord and Saviour. What does this mean? It means commitment to a person in mind and will and heart. It means the commitment of our mind to Jesus Christ, giving as much as we see of ourselves to as much as we see of God revealed in Jesus Christ. Let us start there; we may not understand everything and we never will. But start with Jesus as Lord, don't wait until every doubt is cleared away. Start by saying 'Jesus, I believe in you as the son of God. Lord I believe, help thou mine unbelief.'

And it involves the commitment of the will, the readiness to go wherever the Lord may send us, to become whatever the Lord may ask us to become, the readiness to do whatever the Lord may ask us to do. This is obedience in love. The Lord said to Peter: 'Do you love me? Then feed my sheep, go and work.' Conversion involves the will. Paul said: 'Lord, what would you have me to do?' There is also commitment of the heart. Peter's conversion was not complete until after his failure, his weeping, his forgiveness and his restoration. From that moment on, his heart was broken; but he was grateful.

There are so many people about who are morally decorous but who are not grateful in this sense, because they have never experienced forgiveness. Nearly forty years ago I knelt down with a broken heart, the tears pouring down my face. But I rose knowing that I had been forgiven. From that moment on my heart was full of gratitude and I wanted the world to know about it. I was grateful because I had found forgiveness. Have you? Only you can answer that question. But I beg of you not to by-pass it. The only way to face death unafraid is to find eternal life through acceptance of Jesus Christ *now*.

Here is a prayer: Lord Jesus, you who came to give us abundant, overflowing life, eternal life; help us not to wait for it until our dying day, because if we do we may miss it. Help us to find it now, tonight. Give us the strength to commit ourselves to you, here and now, to you who are the way, the truth and the life. Lord of life, take our lives and give us your eternal, abundant life, now.

* * *

MR. ANDREW CRUICKSHANK

Andrew Cruickshank, a distinguished actor with a long career on the stage to his credit, is also well-known to millions in Britain by his part as Dr. Cameron in the long-running T.V. series 'Dr. Finlay's Casebook'. He is also, in his private life, a keen student of Christian theology and philosophy. On this evening of the mission he was interviewed by Mr. Wynford Vaughan Thomas. The extracts used here are, however, entirely from Mr. Cruickshank's words when he came on to speak before the Bishop's address on 'Learn to Live with Freedom'.

There is no finality about Christianity. It is continual movement. The first great convert was, of course, Paul who recognised in the cross a peculiar symbol of what we are talking about. 'God forbid' he says at the end of Galatians, almost in despair at attempting to explain what the Christian life is: 'God forbid that I should boast of anything save the cross of our Lord Jesus Christ through whom the world is crucified to me, and I to the world.' Paul was writing out of a conviction, a sudden insight. Paul did not know about the crucifixion which we know about. He did not know about the terrifying central cry from the cross. At the third hour Jesus cried out with a loud voice saying *Eloi, eloi, lama sabachthani*, which, translated, means 'My god, my god, why hast thou forsaken me?' The astonishing thing I find about Christianity, as I relate myself to it—I am making no claims about relating anyone else to it—is that there is no more profound sense of the nature of reality than this: that the Son of God, abandoned, is the tremendous revelation of

70

the suffering of the world. So it seems to me, anyway. My recognition of Christ on the cross is, that without this cry, Christ is merely an ethical figure, who can be dismissed as myth or symbol, whatever you like. But this one cry is the point on which the whole thing of Christianity is based, that Christ was a human being, a person. Without this extreme despair of having been rejected by God, there could not be that second cry which comes after it. As Luke says 'At the third hour Jesus cried with a loud voice saying, Father, into thy hands I commit my spirit.' An amazing discovery of the disciples at the resurrection was that Christ was risen. Why? Because in his very life he had conquered himself, lived outwardly to other people. With the resurrection there was a new contagion of love and freedom because, in this recognition and reality, there was no self illusion. The world is a suffering world, and if one is realistic enough to see that, then one will have the courage to hope. Without the suffering, it seems to me, there can be no hope, and we are free entirely to relate ourselves to this figure, illuminating our life . . . it seems to me that basically a Christian's freedom is the freedom to recognise the nature of the man on the cross. In understanding that freedom, one can go on to a new understanding of life. As Paul says, the only thing that matters is new creation.

TOM SHEPHERD
A PERSONAL STATEMENT

Tom Shepherd was an engineer at Rugby at the time of the mission, and is now working in Lincoln. He is in his late-thirties. He was interviewed by the Rev. Peter Larkin, and the interview started with a question as to how he became convinced of the truth of the Christian faith.

'I believe my conversion really started about sixteen years ago when I was at college and I heard the meaning of Christianity explained to me for the first time in my life at a mission. For a long time after that there were periods when I wondered if there was any truth in the account of the resurrection. After a while I came to the stage where I wanted to prove to my own satisfaction that the resurrection was just a story, so that I could live my own life in the way that I wanted to with an easy conscience.

I had already read a fair amount and reasoned about life in general, and this gave me a basis on which to carry on and discover the real truth about Christianity. I read arguments for and against Christianity. I read arguments for and against the resurrection. I reasoned and argued and then, one evening, as I sat alone reading (two and a half years ago), it suddenly occurred to me that no matter how much I reasoned or argued, the resurrection was a fact, and therefore Jesus was the son of God. That evening I became a Christian: I committed my life to Jesus Christ. My reading and reasoning seemed irrelevant. The Holy Spirit had intervened and shown me the wonderful truth.

I find I am far more concerned about other people than I was. I look at other people, most of whom are unaware of God's great love for them, and I think "if only they knew they could be adopted sons of God with the power to be themselves, to live their lives more abundantly, to be better people!" I want to help them to know the truth. The greatest gift I can give to them is to show them God's love in any way that I can.

To be really free is to be the sort of person God wants us to be: not to be ruled by worldly desires: not to be governed by our own fears and anxieties: but to follow Jesus Christ rejoicing in that he has released us from sin.

I do not find that the Christian life is easy; but I never expected it would be. To help me to live this sometimes difficult life the way God wants me to, I need to pray and go to Church and read the Bible regularly. I need especially the holy communion, which is obviously the most important service for the Christian. I used to go to church now and again before my conversion. Sometimes I used to enjoy the hymns, sometimes I used to feel rather guilty and uncomfortable. But now I find the whole thing has taken on a wonderful new meaning, and has become an essential part of my life.'

The Fifth Talk
LEARN TO LIVE WITH FREEDOM

These are remarkable times. I think they could be called an age of revolt, because all through the world, in America, in Europe and in this country we have seen revolt, sometimes led by young people. I believe that all these movements share one factor; they are revolts for freedom against authoritarianism. They are basically a turning against the captivity of material things. For the last fifty years we older people have been preaching a doctrine of man, saying that humanity is getting better and better; more successful, more prosperous, more ingenious, more powerful. But, by ignoring or understressing spiritual values we have let it be thought that getting on, getting rich, getting comfortable is really all that matters, and this concept is being rejected.

Christ said that happiness does not exist in the abundance of material possessions. He said that a man could gain the whole world and lose his own soul. And I believe that young people today are revolting against the dullness and the drabness of a purely material life based upon these misconceptions.

Sometimes these revolts take political forms. But there are other ways. Many people have sought freedom through drugs; some have sought freedom through the casting off of restraints in what has come to be known as the permissive society. Others have sought freedom through this shedding of all responsibility for the people around them. And, let us face it, there are irresponsible people too to be found in many comfortable homes, in surroundings of impeccable respectability, who opt out of life in their own ways; devoting themselves entirely to their own concerns.

But we must not run away from life. We are called to meet it in the power of Christ, whose service is perfect freedom. What we have to do is to discover in what real freedom consists. Real freedom, as we have seen, does not consist in the abundance of material wealth. Wealth begets the fear of losing it, wealth begets bondage, restlessness, the passion to get more and more. There's nothing wrong with having money. The danger is that it can make us close our eyes to the needs of others, to dry up our springs of compassion. One of the most fascinating saints of all time—St. Francis of Assisi—everyman's saint, I like to call him, because maybe we see reflected in him the kind of person we, in our best moments, would like to be, was surrounded in his youth by all that money could buy, living a carefree life. Suddenly he realised it was all ineffective, inadequate, disillusioning. He threw it all over and burst into freedom like a butterfly emerging from the chrysalis, becoming the troubadour of God, the founder of a great order, a lover of all things human and divine.

We cannot buy freedom; we cannot inherit freedom; because freedom does not come naturally. Psychologists tell us that man is by nature a slave from the womb; a slave to his strong inward urges, to his early upbringing, to his environment. Man is not a creature of free choice, but sometimes he thinks himself to be. He cannot manufacture freedom. Education does not give it because it cannot. How then do we acquire this precious thing; this pearl of great price? The way to freedom is through surrender to a power greater than oneself—that is the great point. It is through surrender to Jesus Christ that freedom comes. Dying to self to come alive to him and to others through him. We need to be, and in Christ alone can be, delivered from the many prisons which can hold us.

I once knew a schoolmistress; successful, influential, well-thought of, a driving force, getting to the very top of her profession. But she knew, as middle age approached, that her prison house was ambition, and she threw it all up. People thought her mad when she entered the prison service at a very low salary and for the next twenty years of her life gave her time and affections to young delinquents. She died unpublicised, but loved by all who had found through her a living faith in Jesus Christ.

There is also the prison house of an imperious will, the desire to dominate. I knew of a woman, powerful, determined, devoted to good works, liking her own way. She appeared to run her own life and her family's lives with skill and effectiveness, for she was competent and efficient. Outwardly, everything was very successful, her family bowed to her leadership. But in the process something went out of them, their vitality was sacrificed to her. Although outwardly she appeared to be a very happy person, inwardly she was not so; she was afraid that she might be widowed, that she was going to suffer a painful disease, that the children would cease to depend on her and so forth. She was afraid of loneliness, afraid of being no longer wanted. Then, in the fullness of time, the day came when for her the Lord Jesus ceased to be a remote figure to be summoned in an emergency. He became a living friend, one who could speak to her and speak he did, commanding her to stop trying to run her own life and everybody else's; persuading her to seek his presence and his will, to discover his forgiveness, to find his peace, and to let it flow through her into the lives of others. Very slowly she began to change. People began to notice the difference. She mellowed. The old hardness and dictatorial nature gave way to a quiet strength and a willingness to listen. Today, she is known as a leader. But she is a leader led by God and therefore far more effective and indeed far less dangerous. She has learned the secret of freedom, which begins with a willingness to surrender, to listen, and to obey. There is, too, the prison house of our passions —master urges such as greed, lust, desire for power. We must learn to surrender our passions in the widest sense of that term, to Jesus Christ, asking him to redirect them outwards, into the service of others, because we cannot minister to ourselves and to others at the same time. We need this expulsive power of a new affection for Christ who will redirect our passions into creative outgoing service.

And then there is the prison house of fear; fear of illness, of death, of failure, of being found out. Our Lord wants to set us free; but he will not force. We must open the door. The Lord longs to come in and open the windows to give us a new outlook, a new power, a new purpose. But many of us keep him out because we're scared to let him in. We are scared of the changes he may make in our way of life. There are so many who have never been deeply converted. When we admit Christ into our life we shall find ourselves free from the attitude of keeping ourselves to ourselves. We shall be made to care and to feel and to love and to want to help people. And there is only one place where this can happen, and that is the cross. But the cross is not a sanctuary apart from life. The cross was set up at a meeting point of people, at a meeting point of nations, at a meeting point of races, and Jesus is on that cross because he dared to become involved with people. He dared to care and to reconcile; and the people whom he came to reconcile threw his love back in his face. But it is there, in the hurly-burly of personal encounter and deep involvement, as this tremendous truth illustrates, that Jesus is to be found. He is waiting there to liberate us into the glorious liberty that comes from involvement in the sufferings and needs of the world.

What precisely is he asking us to do? He is asking us to give up the dearest possession we have, the ability to do what we like, as we like, when we like. He is asking us to give up ourselves, in order to come under his leadership, to be at his disposal, to do as he wishes.

There was once a very rich man, highly thought of, a man with a sense of public service, a leader, a Government official of high rank. But he had one fundamental flaw—he was a timid man. Part of him admired Jesus and all that Jesus stood for when the Christ came into his world. He was prepared even to defend him when he was attacked by authority. But he could not bring himself to throw in his lot for Jesus. The days went by, the hour of decision grew very late. Jesus was arrested, condemned and given over to death, and it was then that this man— and maybe by this time you have guessed his name: Joseph of Arimathea—performed three acts of courage: he went to the Roman governor and asked for the dead body of Christ, thereby exposing himself to a similar trial and even death. He went to the cross to take down the corpse and thereby condemned himself among his fellow Jews. He went to his own garden vault which had been carefully kept for his own family, and put the body of the dead carpenter in it. It was in total surrender that this decorously good man found freedom. And so it comes to every one of us. It is through death that we find life. It is through the death of the Christ that we enter into the wonder of the resurrection. And now this prayer.

Lord Jesus, great lover of men, divine Lord and lover, come into the house of my life, come into my heart, come today and stay there, whatever the cost, whatever the change may be.

* * *

NIGHT 6
MR. DEREK NIMMO

Derek Nimmo was another well-known television personality who made a personal contribution to the Coventry Call to Mission. Well-known and popular for his parts in light comedy, he spoke with a seriousness which was in contrast to his professional lightheartedness as seen on stage and screen.

After having spoken of how, in childhood and youth, he

had come to some acceptance of the Christian faith, Mr. Nimmo continued: 'After that I had a complete loss of faith, which happens to so many of us. Then I went to spend a year in Cyprus and I met two remarkable people there who helped me to find my faith again. I spent a small period in a monastery. I found my faith again through reading books by, for example, Paul Tillich, John Robinson, and the Bishop of Coventry. Then I managed to achieve, I think, what I might call an intellectual acceptance of Christ. My thoughts and worries were removed.

I think one of the great things about modern theological writing is the return to the simplicity of the early Church —a return to the simplicity of Christ himself. It seems to me that too much of Christianity is surrounded by man-made doctrine. It is too easy to think of it as just a particular moral code, or a particular conception of God, or a particular method of worship. Christianity is, of course, all these things. But it is much more. And if we are not careful Christ can become lost amongst all the trimmings.

But if you were to ask me what Christianity really means to me, I would invite you to read that remarkable, wonderful, exciting, exhilarating chapter from the Epistle to the Corinthians, Chapter 13, about faith, hope and love. It seems to me that within this chapter is contained the answer to all the questions and the problems that beset mankind, both as individuals and as races, and as nations. If you will let Christ come into your hearts and accept this extremely simple, and yet eternally relevant message which is contained within this chapter, you will be filled with a sense of purpose, a sense of achievement, and you will be truly happier.

St. Paul says: "And now I will show you the best way of all. I may speak in tongues of men or of angels, but if I am without love, I am a sounding gong or a clanging cymbal. I may have the gift of prophecy, and know every hidden truth; I may have faith strong enough to move mountains, but if I have no love, I am nothing. I may dole out all I possess, or even give my body to be burnt, but if I have no love, I am none the better. Love is patient; love is kind and envies no-one. Love is never boastful, nor conceited, nor rude; never selfish, not quick to take offence. Love keeps no score of wrongs; does not gloat over other men's sins, but delights in the truth. There is nothing love cannot face; there is no limit to its faith, its hope, and its endurance. Love will never come to an end. Are there prophets? their work will be over. Are there tongues of ecstacy? they will cease. Is there knowledge? it will vanish away; for our knowledge and our prophecy alike are partial, and the partial vanishes when wholeness comes. When I was a child, my speech, my outlook, and my thoughts were all childish. When I grew up, I had finished with childish things. Now we see only puzzling reflections in a mirror, but then we shall see face to face. My knowledge now is partial; then it will be whole, like God's knowledge of me. In a word, there are three things that last for ever: faith, hope and love; but the greatest of them all is love." [1]

[1] *New English Bible, New Testament.*

MR. CLIFF RICHARD

Cliff Richard, the well-known singer and entertainer, was another public figure who spoke on Youth Night during the Call to Mission. Interviewed by John Moore, Youth Chaplain to the Diocese of Coventry, Mr. Richard spoke, among other things, of how he became a Christian.

He said: 'I suppose I had a fairly easy start in that I have never been an atheist and my family have always believed in God. I remember my father reading the Bible at home and so therefore I have been fairly near to it. But I feel that the big step of becoming a Christian didn't really happen to me until about three and a half years ago. Very briefly, it really began when I was doing a tour of Australia and my father had just previously died. I toyed with the idea of getting in touch with him via a medium, because I was feeling very down, and I wanted to find out, if it was possible, what was in store. A friend of mine . . . who used to read his Bible regularly, pulled a Bible out and I thought "Here it comes!" But I said to him: "You see, my predicament is that I didn't really know whether I should do this. . . ." He flicked over a few pages of the Bible and found three or four places where it actually said to me—because I was the questioner— that I should not dabble in any sort of spirit mediums, but keep clear.

Fortunately, I agreed to take the advice; but what it did do was to start me on the road to reading my Bible again. I began to read the Gospels and particularly John. The one thing that I found I couldn't get away from was that it is all about the man called Christ who is claimed to be the Son of God, who is claimed to have died for our sins. I had to do something about it. To be a person who can call himself a Christian, I had to do something. . . . From what I have learned in the past three or four years particularly there are a few things, it seems to me, that make a Christian. A Christian is to believe very specially that Jesus was a man here on earth, that he was, moreover, the Son of God, that he died specifically for man's sins, and that Jesus Christ lived again. I think one great thing about Christianity is that we have a living saviour in someone who is alive and very much working today. But, believing these things, I still felt there was a thin line which stops people being Christians. That goes when one says: "Alright, Jesus Christ, I believe these things about you; I want you to take over my life." Until I did that, three and a half years ago, I feel that I was not a Christian. . . .

I mention this business about feeling down in the dumps about my career and other things. Now it may seem rather trivial in the light of the problems of the world. But it was my particular problem at the time, and the problem was eliminated almost immediately. Also my outlook on my career, I feel, is far more healthy now because reading the Bible shows us that our life on earth can be used to glorify God, whether one is a singer or anything else. It's been a great help to me to know that I can glorify God in what I do.'

Asked what he would say to young people who found prayer and Bible reading and church participation difficult, Mr. Richard replied: 'I think it is very important to get in with a group of other young people who are finding it just as difficult as you are. I am a fairly young Christian, three and a half years standing isn't really that long, and I still find it's never easy. I think it is best to get in with a church group who are also studying systematically through a certain chapter or a certain book of the Bible. This is really the only way, because we have to learn before we can grow as Christians. . . .

The thing about Christianity is that it demands much from each one of us . . . but when it suddenly becomes important to you and you realise that you need it desperately, then you find time for it. Until we get our minds in the right perspective, we will never really get anywhere. One suddenly realises that one *can* find time. I think I have one of the busiest lives. Show-Biz people don't lead a regular life, so you never know what's going to happen tomorrow. But I desperately wanted Christ, so I found and made time for him, and I think anybody who is serious about Christian faith has got to approach it in this way. One has got to think seriously about it and make room for it in one's life.'

The Sixth Talk
TO YOUTH

As I look around this vast audience tonight, I think there may be one thing which I have done more of than any single person among the eight thousand present, and that is more flying in aircraft! During the past twenty years I have flow thousands and thousands of miles, North America, Africa, India, Asia, Australia and all parts of Europe time and time again. Sometimes I have flown by night and I have looked down upon a world spread out beneath, seeing here and there lights, but for the rest, darkness. And I think this is a picture of the world today: the thrilling, exciting, interesting world, a world of scientific advance, a world of power and progress, but in so many ways a world of darkness, rife with wars, hunger, refugees, a strange mixed-up world full of strange, mixed-up people.

When an aircraft is flying through the night it is guided by, among other things, radio beacons. Now I believe that as a nation we are heading off course because of wrong signals along our way. What are some of these faulty beacons by which we are supposed to be guided? Here are a few.

First, the idea of having a good time is the only thing that matters. I'm all in favour of getting a kick out of life, but we need to make sure that it is the right kind of kick. If we live merely for pleasure, the party is bound to end, sooner or later. There is always the morning after the night before, and this kind of living just for pleasure will yield a kick for a time. But that quickly runs out. A second false beacon is over concentration on sex. Sex feelings are one of God's greatest gifts to mankind; but at present we seem to be almost obsessed by this part of life. We have it thrown at us from screens, from print and the impression is being widely put across that if only we freely follow our urges in this respect, we shall be free and content. But it just does not work out that way. Wisely used sex can be the greatest creative force in the world. Wrongly used it can be terribly destructive. Another false navigation beacon is the idea that to get and to spend is the sum total of all existence. Recently I went to the theatre. As I sat down my companion nudged me and said: 'Look, there's the richest man in Europe.' I looked; I had never seen a more miserable face in all my life. If getting and spending of money brings happiness, then all I can say is that that man and a lot of other very rich people do not reflect it in their faces.

And there's a fourth false navigation beacon—the idea

that the only people that matter are those who get to the top: who make friends and influence people and get into positions of power. There's an awful lot of loneliness at the top and the faces of those who get there—wherever the top is—are often tired and strained, worried and frightened. There's nothing particularly wrong in ambition, or in a desire to get on—wherever 'on' is—but don't be fooled into thinking that getting to the top automatically brings contentment. It can bring frustration and loneliness.

Another false navigation beacon is the idea that the getting of qualifications is all that matters. Society begins to judge a person not by his character but by the number of technical qualifications that he possesses. In other words, a man is judged by his price, and not by his value. A person with many technical qualifications is not necessarily a happy person, and the purpose of education is not to be found exclusively in the getting of intellectual qualifications; but rather in the development of character. True education should give a goal for life that is satisfying and creative in the service of other people.

A nation steering by these false lights has no future, because it is on a wrong course and bound for trouble. All these false beacons for individuals and for countries lead sooner or later to disaster. Very few of you are old enough to remember the last war. But that was a time when we as a nation had three true beacons: someone to look up to; an adventure to live for, and a goal to work for. We had someone to look up to in Winston Churchill. His voice stimulated men into action, calling many to brave living. I know all this may sound very old hat to you younger people; but it was very real to us. We had an adventure to live for. We stood alone for a while—our little island against the greatest armed force the world had ever seen. We alone, for a time, were defending the free world against the secret police, concentration camps, the gas chamber and all the horrors of the Nazi regime of long ago. And we had a goal, something to work for. Every single one of us knew in our hearts that the only thing that really mattered then was victory and peace, and we were prepared to work long days and nights to achieve it. Yet all this was only on a material level. And war is evil, anyway. These high motivations can be found in a far finer framework than that. So I want to put before you someone to look up to, an adventure to live for, a goal to work for. The person to look up to is Jesus; the adventure is the life that he came to bring to every one of us, the goal is the service of God and mankind. But we must find a power, and know where we can find it.

I am going to be very personal now. One day many years ago I met a man who knew Jesus as a friend, in spirit and in truth. He knew him not just as an example from the past, but as a living person. He knew him as a source of power. I met this man at a party, when he stood out among all the rest of the people: there was a light in his eyes and I knew at once that here was a man who had clearly found a faith that worked. I was intrigued and captured. So when he asked me to go along and talk in his house, I accepted gladly. Eventually, I found myself telling him that I had nothing to live for, I had found nothing to grip my energies. And he told me how Jesus Christ had become real to him through an honest facing of his own failures and weakness and compromises. As he talked, I began to feel rather uncomfortable, because I knew I was impressionable and changeable, according to the company I was in. I knew full well that I was a pagan among the pagans, a semi-religious among the religious. This can be hard going, because you always have to try

The Settlers bring their message to Coventry Cathedral

Quintin Hogg opens his case

Andrew Cruickshank responds to questions from Wynford Vaughan-Thomas

Derek Nimmo as himself

to remember which company you are in. I was trying to serve three masters, enjoyment, popularity and religion, and I knew that, basically, I was a coward, unwilling and unable to do what I knew the Christian life was really calling me to do.

So I knelt down. And I gave as much as I saw of myself to as much as I saw of God revealed for me in Jesus Christ. Immediately I found forgiveness. I knew that a weight had fallen away and I found a strange, inward peace. I learned that an experiment of obedience issues as an experience of discovery. The Lord ceased to be a remote person and became alive. I began to discover that he was the friend who never lets one go, never lets one down, and never lets one off.

And he gave me something to live for, and has done ever since. The Christian life is a thrillingly adventurous life. So what are you going to do with your life? Wrap it up in cotton wool? Or are you going to offer yourselves to the Lord of all good life and go out in the spirit of adventure to serve? If you become a real Christian, God may call some of you to the furthest corners of the world. Others he may call to service here at home. He will call some of you to the choice of an adventurous career. Others will find adventure to the most ordinary career. But the Christian adventure can be discovered every single day, if we listen to what God has to say to us. For he will talk, provided we listen and obey.

And he gives us a goal; self-fulfilment through the service of God and our fellow men. The building of the kingdom of God. This is hard reality. It means going out in his name and with his power to put people right with God, to put people right with one another, to put right the evil conditions of society. It is a call to a non-stop life of constant service and action and adventure.

4

87

Most of you are going to get married someday. The marriage service includes two words: 'I will'. You don't drift into marriage; it is a commitment, a contract, a giving of mind and will and heart to another person. So, in precisely the same way, the Christian life starts with a surrender or commitment of our mind and will and heart —and it usually starts with the will. 'Lord, I am willing to go wherever you may send me, do whatever you may ask me to do, to become whatever you may ask me to become. Lord, I am willing.' Dare you say those words? Don't wait until all your questions and intellectual difficulties have been ironed out, until you are older, or whatever. The longer you wait to become a Christian, the harder it will be. How much in the meantime you will be missing! How much other people will miss through you because you are not a Christian! So why not say to Christ: 'Lord, I am prepared to give as much as I know of myself to as much as I see of you, revealed in Jesus Christ'?

Most of all important is the giving of our hearts. There is a story of an American boy brought up in a very good home; but it was one from which he intended to shake loose. So he came over to Europe. After a while, his life, in various ways, went way off the rails, and he never wrote home because he felt ashamed. Gradually he went down-hill and down, until one day he came to himself and decided to go home. He arrived at night. It was dark. He found the back door was open, so he went up the stairs and into his room where he discovered, to his astonishment, the bedclothes had been turned down. He thought this was very strange as indeed it was. Were they expecting a visitor? Anyway, he took a chance and got into bed. In the morning, he woke up, hearing footsteps coming up the stairs, and his father's voice saying: 'Time to get up, son!' He wondered how his father knew that he was home, got out of bed, opened the door, and saw his father at the bottom of the stairs. There was a moment of intense silence, then they went to meet each other and shake hands.

Well, forty years ago I heard the words, metaphorically speaking, 'It's time to get up, son', and I found that my little act of commitment was met by the most wonderful commitment of God to me. My 'I will' was met by his 'I will come to you'. In the last book of the Bible we read: 'Behold, I stand at the door and knock; if any man will open I will come in and make my abode with him.' I believe that God is knocking at the door of your life to-night; open it and you will find that he will come in.

* * *

NIGHT 7
LADY CHICHESTER

Sir Francis Chichester, yachtsman and pilot, caught the imagination of the world when he successfully sailed alone round the world in his yacht, Gipsy Moth, in 1966–67. On the seventh night of the Call to Mission she attended, with Sir Francis, and, interviewed by Ronald Allison, spoke of her Christian faith and what it had meant to her.

She said: 'I was born into a Christian family, baptised as one and brought up as one. I was educated at a convent at Wantage and this all helped and strengthened me. My faith is that if you have faith in God, which gives you purpose in living, you have faith in yourself and faith in your fellow-men, and the rest follows.'

Asked whether the greatest test of her faith had not been when Sir Francis was making his round-the-world voyage, she replied:

'The greatest test of my faith was not at that time. I think I should let you know, because this is a great story of Christian healing. He was very ill before any of this sailing, and I had to make the decision, against other people's opinions, but I set my course and I definitely had divine guidance as to what to do, and in time he recovered and was able to do the first solo race. I can truly say that I was more pleased at his return to health than the fact that he won it.'

Asked whether, during the time that Sir Francis Chichester was sailing round the world, she was praying for him or whether she was confident all the time, Lady Chichester replied: 'I was absolutely confident. Sometimes I was surprised at myself that I never worried. But I am a cautious person and I believe in the dedication of a yacht, and this was done by the Rev. Tubby Clayton at a wonderful little service we had in the presence of twelve friends. During my life I've had friends who will always pray when I ask them and who believe, as I do, that prayer is an output of power, and very, very strong when it is joined together in faith. And so I sent twenty prayer-cards, all over the world, and these people prayed for him. There were millions praying for him by the time he came into Plymouth, including many young children. . . . I think this inspired them and really gave them something worth-while. I used to go to sleep at night and think, "How extraordinary, I am not worrying." Even when he capsized, and I was the first one to be told, I was absolutely calm.

Finally, when Lady Chichester was asked what she felt people without Christian faith were missing, she said:

'I feel they miss a framework, for one thing. And life must be very empty for them. Unless they have this faith which I have and this power of prayer which is so real and can be used through daily prayer and meditation and study, I do feel that they miss an awful lot. And I would like to sum up in the words of a prayer, prayed hundreds of years ago by St. Augustine of Hippo. "Thou hast made us for thyself, and our hearts are restless till they find rest in thee." I think that sums it up.'

PETER WORSLEY
A PERSONAL STATEMENT

Peter Worsley, the son of a clergyman in the diocese of Coventry, is a physical education instructor, active in Christian youth work.

I can consider myself very fortunate in that I have been brought up in a Christian home and have been encouraged to attend church since an early age. I was confirmed at fifteen, and I can well remember that at this age I became very respectful of the Christian faith and its standards. It was not until some four years later that I came to find for myself the joy which Christians have in their lives when they invite Christ into their hearts and ask him to rule their lives and live by his standards. At the age of nineteen I spent a week of my holiday assisting in the cook-house of a church society's camp for teenage boys. I was working in a strange place, and with strangers, and yet I found it easy to make new friends among the campers, and it was through seeing the joy of Christian living in the lives of my friends there that I came to ask the Lord Jesus Christ to come into my own life.

These friends at the camp had shown me by their example that Christ is not a vague figure in history; but a living saviour and friend, and I became anxious to make this reality my own. In the same way that Simon Peter, that rough man and fisherman-disciple, fell on to his knees before Christ and confessed his sins, so I asked forgiveness for my sins and I asked God to use my life in his service. I rose from my knees in the wonderful knowledge that my burden of sin had been lifted, and that I had been granted a new lease of life.

Without my faith in God and obedience to his will, I would still be leading the selfish aimless existence of my pre-christian days. Because I have accepted God's son, Jesus Christ, as my saviour, I have found a very real strength in his promises to help me cope with the process of living.

Jesus, I believe, leads us out of the things which cramp or deform our lives, because his is the only power which can transform us into better human beings. God wants each one of us to invite his son into our lives; but he has given us free will and therefore he leaves us to make this decision for ourselves. Although my faith in God has been put to trial by problems in life, he has always given me strength to cope with these same problems, and I am keeping to my decision to give Jesus Christ the first place in my life.

Now that my way of living and my emotions are directed towards following the example and teaching of Christ, my life has purpose and satisfaction and I have found a joy in living which surpasses anything else which this world has to offer me. Christ is a reality to me and my relationship with him is a personal one. For many people a purpose in life is a fortune worth finding. My purpose is to try to live my life by the perfect moral standards of Jesus, standards of honesty, kindness, humility, brotherly love and so on.

These are the hall marks of those friends who led me to the Lord. I have seen in these friends, and I now know for myself, the joy of being a Christian. I find that God continues to help me solve my problems and I simply put my trust in him and I ask him to rule my life entirely. . . .

I might add from my own personal experience of Christian living that, where God and love are, there is happiness and contentment of mind. The way to happiness is to keep your mind free from hate, to keep yourself free from worry, to expect little, to give much, to forget self, to think of others. It may be thought that there is nothing new in this philosophy. But there is something new in it if you've never tried it. Life means vitality, and Christians, who get their vitality from God, find, as I have found, that God's power creates happiness and purposeful living. It gives the desire to bring others to experience the same joy in their lives.

The Seventh Talk
LEARN TO LIVE WITH A PURPOSE

In the last two nights there have been brought together here over fifteen thousand people to hear the Gospel. Last night, in that unforgettable youth gathering, four hundred young people stayed behind to commit their lives to Jesus Christ, to accept him as Saviour and Lord, and to go out into his service into the world of today. I thank God for the quite wonderful way, also, in which all our remaining debts for the cost of this mission are being met.

The subject for this evening is 'Living with Purpose'. There are great numbers of people who appear to be living without any purpose whatever, and I think it is true of our nation as a whole at this present time. We seem to have lost direction. And because of this, the subject of tonight's meeting is of first-rate importance. I think there are three kinds of people living in the world today: the drifters, with no overriding loyalty, no allegiance to anybody or anything and no consuming passion. A lady came up to me last night and said: 'Before this call to mission began I felt flat, my faith had died on me, and now I've found a new refreshment and a purpose.'

Two days before I heard of a young priest who had lost his faith and was about to give up his ministry. He came rather critically and unwillingly to the first meeting last Tuesday, and by the end he had found his faith again. Now he is going forward into the ministry with deep conviction. Praise God for all these things.

Again there are people with inadequate, passing loyalties. I remember reading somewhere these words: 'Everyone is guided by something. What are you guided by?' Is it your desires, your bank balance, your wife, your husband, what the neighbours think? If you are guided by those things then your life is turned inwards. You have ambition of a sort, but the wrong sort and an inadequate sort. You are worshipping yourself. On the other hand, and in sharp contrast, there are people who are governed and directed by a divine purpose, who have caught something of the love of God and who are reflecting it and passing it on. Such people with a divine purpose in their lives are to be met often in the Bible. One of those who can be described as a man with a divine purpose was

Jeremiah. Shy, timid, retiring, only wanting to remain on the circumference of life if he could, he yet held that he was caught up into a divine plan. It was this discovery of God's plan which led him out of what could have been a quiet, peaceful but useless existence and hurled him into the maelstrom of international affairs. Jeremiah lived through four reigns. Constantly, he was a bringer of bad news, of warnings from God to his nation. With courage, this intrepid man appeared before kings and rulers, high priests, crowds, telling them in stark terms that if they went on with their present way of life, worshipping false gods, denying the validity of the true god, there was only one possible destiny awaiting them and that was national destruction. They laughed, they mocked, they ridiculed, they persecuted. They tortured him, letting him down once into a pit so that the mire was right up to his waist and from which place he was rescued only at the last moment. Yet all the time this shy, retiring man went on delivering God's message. He became one of the greatest prophets of all. What he prophesied, moreover, came true: the nation was destroyed. But even then he went with its people into exile and he died in exile. A failure? No! He is recognised as one of the great prophetic voices of all time, a man with a divine purpose.

And now let's take some instances from our own age. Some years ago a man well known to me emerged from service in the Air Force with his health shattered, a chip on his shoulder, a dislike of the Church and a disbelief in God. But God moves in a mysterious way, as has often been said. His sister-in-law, aged fifteen, developed cancer. But such was her radiant faith in Christ that she bore her sufferings with wonderful peace and joy. I came into this when, one day, my phone rang and I was asked to go to a country church to confirm this girl's brother-in-law,

this very ex-Air Force man. He had been completely captured by the faith he had seen in this young girl. When
I entered the church there, sitting in the front row,
propped up with cushions, her face pale but with the
look of an angel, sat this girl. We did not know that she
had only three more weeks to live. Next to her was this
crippled man whose health had been shattered. I confirmed him. As I walked out a very tough Irish doctor
came up to me and said: 'That girl ought to be dead by
now, or suffering agony, and what do I see? I see a
saint!' Within three days that doctor himself was converted. When the girl died almost the whole village came
to the church and that was the beginning of a new life for
the young man from the Air Force. He went with his
wife to another village where there was a church congregation of twenty-five. Within a year that congregation
had grown to two hundred and fifty because a man and
wife had an open home and open hearts, and because their
faith was so contagious. The years went by and I asked
the couple to come into this diocese to run the Retreat
House. This they did, and did it well. And then one night
the blow fell. I was taking a conference which ended in the
Service of Compline, and when it was over we walked
out of the chapel, but the wife did not move. She had a
heart attack and died shortly after that service. Just for
three days that man's faith was shaken, but it held firm in
the end and today he is still a man of tremendous faith.
His soul marches on in his battered body, which is in
continuous pain from morning to night. One day he was
arguing with some opponents and at the end he said to
them: 'You know, it's just no good you people saying to me
that Christ was a myth. I know him because I have met him.'

And now a story with a very different kind of a character. A woman with an acute mind and a powerful

personality, she was carving out a successful career after obtaining an excellent university degree. Then she entered into a transforming experience of the love of Jesus Christ. Her character was mellowed without being made soft, and she was led to give up political ambitions to become the editor of a Christian newspaper, into which she poured all her intellectual gifts. Next, the Lord spoke to her, asking her to go and teach difficult children. So she went, and after three months was desperate—she was failing dismally. Then one day she started from where they were. She asked: 'What *are* you interested in?' She found that they were interested in simple, human, basic problems: how to get on with the boy-friend, how to get on with their parents, and so forth. 'But' she said, 'that is exactly what God is interested in.' And so God came alive to those children through that woman. Later there was a local election and she stood as a candidate, after much heart-searching. She was accepted and elected. Today she is using all her Christian knowledge and her enthusiasm to give mature Christian leadership.

Important lessons emerge from these stories. The total unexpectedness, both as to timing and as to the manner of God's demands upon our life: a toughening, rather than a softening of life when we find God's purpose: and the fact that, as a result, we are thrown into significant contacts with people. The Christian life is not an escape from the world. It is not an insurance policy against suffering. It is not an individualistic, pietistic exercise. It is not primarily concerned with morals; but with the one supreme moral demand to love. The Christian life is not a vague existence, but the discovery that God has a purpose for each one of us. But the discovery of God is only the first stage. The discovery of God's purpose for our life is the all-important second stage. But we must realise that this revelation of God's plan and purpose does not usually burst upon us like a meteor from the sky. It may start very small, like an acorn which eventually grows to an oak.

But how do we find God's purpose and plan for our life? I would say: be willing to be shown. When I was a young man at Oxford I went, once, to call on the head of the college and there I met Field Marshal, as he later became, Smuts. He was a great man in his day. In the course of two minutes he turned to me and he said: 'Young man, what are you going to do with your life?' I have never forgotten that. I think God is saying to us all something similar: 'What are we going to do with our lives?' The first words of the converted Saul, on the road to Damascus, let it be remembered were: 'Lord, what would you have me to *do*?'

It is essential to deal immediately with the answer given us by God. And to be alert to his still small voice. Elijah was told by God to do three things, and in the doing of them he changed the nation. Philip, in the Book of Acts, was told to go to the main road and he would be shown what to do. He arrived there and found a man reading a book. It was the scriptures, and the man could not understand what he was reading, even though he was a high official at the court of Candace, the Queen of Ethiopia. Philip explained it to him and this resulted in the opening up of the Christian faith to another nation. Paul was wondering where to go when he heard his friend Luke, the doctor, say to him in a dream: 'Come into Macedonia and help us.' Paul went, and the whole of Europe opened up to the Christian gospel. A very small beginning, but with very great results.

A friend of mine was told by God to go and spend the night on the Embankment in London. There he found a vagrant and through him was introduced to another world: the world of suffering and of the lost and of the drop-out. He went with that man to the crypt of St. Martin-in-the-Field and as a result of what he saw his life was changed. Today he is a priest. Some people come to involvement with Jesus through involvement with the world. Some people come to involvement with the world through involvement with Jesus. But they both end in the same place—in obedience to Jesus Christ.

God is waiting upon every single one of us. God has a plan and a purpose for every single life. He can make every one of us part of the divine plan for reshaping his world, and you and I will be restless until we have discovered and obeyed and embarked upon God's purpose for our life. Young or old, rich or poor, with five talents or only one, it does not matter in the least to God what we are or what we have. Somebody once said: 'There is no entrance fee into the Kingdom of Heaven, but the annual subscription is everything you've got.' Those are true words. So I would say to you now, don't procrastinate, don't leave it until another day. Don't say I will wait awhile, and come back another time. It may be too late, later. God wants all of us now. He wants to take control of our lives now, and to give as much as we know of ourselves to as much as we see of God in Christ—now. We must start where we are. It will not be an easy life. It is never easy. But, to use Biblical language: 'My grace is sufficient for you.'

So often we are told to look up at the cross. We are sometimes told to try and look out from behind the cross, at the world, and to see that world through the eyes of Jesus and to feel that world with the heart of Jesus. Seeing and feeling its sufferings, knowing some of its homeless and hungry, knowing some of its empty souls and loveless homes. When we do that we shall find that we are involved in situations where the Lord is always at work, and we shall be caught up into that stream of love, that on-going mission of his, and will find that he will give us a new direction and purpose. We shall indeed then begin to 'live with purpose'.

* * *

NIGHT 8
MRS. JOANNA KELLEY

Mrs. Joanna Kelley, after a distinguished career in the Prison Serivce, during which she was at one time Governor of Holloway, is now Assistant Director in charge of Womens Establishments at the Home Office. She is also a member of the Archbishops' Council of Evangelism. She was interviewed on this night by Tom Coyne, and what follows is a digest of that interview.

Mrs. Kelley was asked, first of all, whether she thought it mattered today as to whether a person was a Christian or not. She replied: 'I think it matters possibly more than ever, because I think it is the only hope for humanity. I do not think there is any chance of our race of mankind surviving unless we can learn to become Christians, with a Christian sense of values, with Christian thoughts towards each other, with all the teachings that Christ taught us. I don't necessarily mean being Church people. I mean really following Christ and trying to be like him . . . One of the things that worries me is, I think, that the churches tend to make Christianity a thing of the past; a thing of history; set, and not living. They make it a religion. But Christianity is not a religion: it's a way of life: a new life, becoming a new person. You may worship God in beautiful buildings. You may worship him in one way or another, and all ways are good; but you've got to do more than come to Church: you've got to be a completely different kind of human being.'

Asked whether she had ever had her faith tested, Mrs. Kelley replied: 'I suppose we all have, and, of course, if you work in prisons you see tremendous sadness and tragedy. As the result of sin you see man bent and all gone astray, perhaps more than most people.' When asked whether it had been her experience that people in prison were sometimes helped by the Christian message, Mrs. Kelley said: 'I think there is one thing about being in prison: perhaps for the first time in life people come to a sense of need. They have been through a terrible experience: they have been found out in some mean and shabby sin; they have been put into a dock, judged by their fellow-men and found wanting, and so they come to prison feeling very humiliated and debased. Sometimes for the very first time in their lives they have a sense of need. "All is not well with me." "What is wrong?" And, of course, it is the hungry who can be filled. This is the moment when the Christian message of hope and forgiveness can really come into a person's heart because that heart is open to it.'

Mrs. Kelley was reminded that the theme of the evening was 'Learn to live with power', and she was asked what she meant, personally, by 'power'. She replied: 'I mean by power, the power of the Holy Spirit, and all power is of God. You may abuse power, or you may use it well. But you are an instrument of power and power is of God. We are told the Holy Spirit is the Lord and giver of life. Life seems to me to be sometimes like a swift, strong river flowing to the sea. If you throw yourself in and go with the current of life then you live with power. It does sometimes seem to me very extraordinary that when one knows this one doesn't always do it. One should always pray before speaking and pray before acting. When you do, things do go so much better.'

STUART BELL
A PERSONAL STATEMENT

A graduate in theology of Exeter University, Stuart Bell at the time of the mission was gaining experience in industry before going on to train for the ministry.

In the last five years since I have been a Christian I have experienced God not as some ethereal distant being; but as a personal and powerful friend.

I was twelve when I first heard that God had a demand to make upon my life. This was a double demand in that, not only had he created me and given me life, but also he had sent Jesus to die for me. The most natural thing that I could think of was to try to do something that would please God—something that would pay him back for all the things that he had done for me. So I resolved, as best I could, to turn over a new leaf, to help at home, to be obedient, to go to church and so forth. I tried to work my way to heaven. I wanted to earn favour with God.

But somehow, through all this time, I did not find that I was drawn any closer to him, or that I had any kind of relationship with him. By the end of the year I realised that despite all this activity I had failed to get to God, but all the same he still made a demand upon my life—the demand of total commitment to him.

Because of this failure, I determined to bury my head in the sand: I tried to avoid God, and in actual fact, I changed my church. At this time I was growing up. I wanted to throw away every kind of authority and live my own life in my own way. I was at the age when I was becoming aware of new desires. I wanted to be able to give full expression to them all. In a funny way, I found myself living a double life: I was one person at school and another person at home during the week-end. I discovered within myself a very real tension between good and bad. I still tried, even at this stage, occasionally to turn over a new leaf; but finished up just as before, doing exactly what I wanted to do without regard for anyone or anything.

When I was seventeen I suddenly began to realise what the truth was about Christianity. I honestly don't know how this happened. I can't tell, even today. I think God must have brought to the forefront of my mind things I had heard in the church I had abandoned years before. I was not at any big meeting like tonight; but entirely on my own when the full realisation of the death of Jesus came alive to me. I became aware of the fact that I couldn't earn my way to heaven, that I couldn't work myself into a relationship with God. I became aware of the fact that all this time what had separated me from God was the things that I had done wrong—my whole sinful nature. But alongside this came the realisation that Jesus himself had borne the punishment for my sins when he was crucified; whereas I should have been punished for them, Jesus died in my place. There was nothing for me to do except to confess my sins to Jesus and ask him to come into my life.

The Eighth Talk
LEARN TO LIVE WITH POWER

All over this country there are power lines. You cannot see power; but if you touch one of those lines you will quickly know all about it! And so it is with the power of God. Christians call it the power of the Holy Spirit and, by the mercy of God, this wonderful power is an offering which God makes to us. This life-changing power can be ours. The early Christians had it, without a doubt. Read the Book of the Acts as though you had never read it before and you will find the most fantastic stories of conversions and healings and reconciliations are there on record. Those very ordinary people were made very extraordinary by the power of the spirit and they turned the world upside down. This is the power which can un-freeze the soul, and many certainly need unfreezing, including those of some outwardly committed Christians.

From the very earliest days of the Bible, men and women have been conscious of power in this sense. In the Old Testament the power of the spirit was thought of as superhuman, mysterious elusive, like the wind of the desert whipping the sand into new shapes. It was thought of as a force coming in from outside, no-one knew from whence, and bringing with it changes which no man could foretell. It was in that power that Samson was able to slay lions, to overcome men, and to break ropes asunder. It was that power which was referred to when it was said of David, after his anointing by Samuel; 'The spirit of the Lord came mightily upon David, from that day forward.' It was something from which people could not escape. And so throughout the whole of the Old Testament the spirit of God is a power that is exciting and dynamic. In the New Testament it is given a different interpretation. There, the spirit of power is seen as coming not just to prophets, or to anointed kings, or to the particularly chosen from age to age, but it is shown as coming up on all men and women, however humble, who could say from the bottom of their hearts 'Jesus is Lord'. So in the New Testament we see the spirit of God battling against the forces of evil, described by Paul in terms of 'principalities and powers in high places', and we see this spirit also raising the potential of ordinary men and women far beyond that which it otherwise would have been.

This Lord, the spirit, created a new fellowship of people who had moved out from individualism and security into a great fellowship united in the spirit of God. It became, as I have said, ordinary people doing extraordinary things together. The spirit which had been so markedly at work in Jesus during his earthly ministry began to come in, as he had promised, enabling his followers to do marvellous things. Enabled by the power of the holy spirit, those early Christians were able to bear their witness. Incidentally, the word 'martyr' means a witness. This high voltage, incalculable power is very different from what one might call the 'mini-spirit' tamed and shrunken in that Victorian hymn:

> And his that gentle voice we hear
> Soft as the breath of even
> That checks each fault and calms each fear
> And speaks of heaven.

105

The true nature of the Holy Spirit is to be found much more fully and richly expressed in the *Veni Creator*:

> Come Holy Ghost our souls inspire,
> And lighten with celestial fire;
> Thou the anointing spirit art
> Who dost thy sevenfold gifts impart:
> Anoint and cheer our soiled face
> With the abundance of thy grace.

What does the Holy Spirit do to a man? First of all, he gives a man vitality. There is all the difference in the world between existing and living. Our materialistic, twentieth century way of life is often sadly deficient in this respect. If we are going to demonstrate as Christians more effectively the power of the Holy Spirit to young people especially, then we need the power of God so that those who encounter us take notice. Jesus said to Nicodemus, a highly intelligent person, who was seeking after a power the nature of which he did not understand, or at any rate the price for which he did not understand; 'Unless a man is born again he cannot see the Kingdom of God.' Nicodemus replied, 'Can a man enter a second time into his mother's womb and be born?' Christ came straight back at him: 'In truth I tell you, no-one can enter the Kingdom of God without being born of water and spirit. Flesh can only give birth to flesh, it is spirit which gives birth to spirit.'

Again, the Holy Spirit makes possible a new relationship with God. Until then, maybe, the relationship has been remote. But the Holy Spirit brings the relationship closer and with it the responsibility to respond to a God close at hand who makes demands. Much of our Christian life is a response to the action of God, bringing with it the obligations to use our time, our talents, our money, our effort—all that we have in the service of God. One of the phrases I love most in the Bible is 'alive unto God'. Dead to sin, alive unto God, in union with Jesus Christ—that is what we need to be.

Thirdly, the Holy Spirit brings a new sense of responsibility to others. We begin to see other people as people of significance and value in the eyes of God. We begin to see people in a new light; people in need; people we have never noticed before; people with great potential for good. We begin to see people often as shot through with God. And this brings a new sense of responsibility for life and for everybody around us.

Fourthly, the Holy Spirit brings us a new sense of necessity for service. The Holy Spirit comes not so much to individuals, let it be remembered, as to individuals in community. What is more, the Holy Spirit is still as dynamic and creative and at work as he ever was. He is at work in art, in science and wherever human energy is used for the extension of knowledge and the betterment of mankind.

And now I put a question to you. In what way does your own faith lack this vitality and power that was so evident in the Book of the Acts? It is a question we should all ask ourselves often. Those early Christians did not just know about God: they knew God. God ceased to be remote and became one who is found at the heart of life, discoverable in prayer, so that prayer became a great experience of contact with God. He was found in worship, so that worship was found a tremendously overwhelming experience of contact with God. He was found in fellowship so that in fellowship together they found God. Above all, perhaps, he was found in service, as they went out to serve and to witness. So, too, can we find him.

We shall find him as we discover a new responsibility

to one another. It was asked in the Bible: 'Am I my brother's keeper?' The answer for all of us is yes, I am. If there was famine in Jerusalem it was the responsibility of the Christians in Corinth and Ephesus to meet it. If there is poverty and hunger and suffering anywhere it is your responsibility and mine to do something about it and to make our influence felt upon that situation in whatever ways we find open to us, because we are brothers in God with those who suffer.

The Holy Spirit of God also brings deliverance. How we need this! In the days of the early Christians it was deliverance from superstition, from blind faith and blind chance. Today, the circumstances are a little different. Our great need today is deliverance from the sense of uselessness, of hopelessness, and of the inevitability of decline and ultimate disaster which is the canker gnawing at the hearts of many people today, even if the fact of it is unacknowledged. One of the things most prevalent today is this very sense that, as it were, there is no purpose in anything. The Holy Spirit delivers us out of this sense of hopelessness into the liberty and splendour of the children of God. In the early Church, its members were not perfect. Many of those Christians in those first centuries were stupid, obstinate, mixed-up, just like their twentieth-century successors, for that matter. Even so, there is as a fact this strange power running through every page of the Book of the Acts. Why? Because the early Church prayed with expectancy that this power would come, and come it did, in accordance with the promises of our Lord himself.

But the Holy Spirit does not come into our lives without cost, for when he is really in control, we are no longer our own masters. We are taken whither we know not. We are often asked to do things which, humanly speaking, we could not do in our own strength. God will be our strength. We shall be continually confronted with the unexpected and each end of the day will be the beginning of an exciting new day in which the Holy Spirit will lead us out into the lives of other people, and give us the power and the words and the wisdom through which to help others to find, through Jesus Christ, the way to live.

* * *

NIGHT 9
THE RT. HON. QUINTIN HOGG

The Rt. Hon. Quintin Hogg PC, MP, *formerly Lord Hailsham, Member of Parliament and Privy Councillor, has had a notable career in public life and in politics. He is also an eminent barrister.*

You have asked me to speak tonight on 'Living in Christ'. I am an unsuitable character, you may think, to select for this vital subject, and you would be right. Two reasons only persuaded me to venture. The one was selfish, the other more reputable. The selfish reason was that I had long wished to see this famous Cathedral church, famous for its architecture, for its dramatic history, and above all because it is in the life of this nation, in its very fabric, the symbol of our belief in rebirth during this life and resurrection after death.

Have you ever pondered upon the paradox of our presence here, and upon the paradox of Christianity in history? For my second reason—reputable, I think—is my belief that in this time and this age what is at stake is not religious orthodoxy, or traditional piety; but the very continued existence of Christianity and its influence on the world. What a paradox its influence has been, that five thousand people should actually come together two thousand years later because of their relationship with a man who lived, and died, two thousand years ago. He made small impact upon the Roman Empire in his life, and little enough upon the Jewish worlds. In most of the planet he was unknown. Like Socrates, he left no written word of his own, and the only writing of which we hear was a doodle, scribbled in the dust. He is scarcely mentioned a generation later. He died in public, and if he rose, he appeared only to his followers and so in private.

But, of course, the answer to the question is simple. After two thousand years, his followers believe, as they have done from the start, that Jesus is still alive, not simply as Shakespeare is still alive in Hamlet, not as Socrates was still alive through the works of his disciples who wrote: but alive as we are alive, really and truly living. And apart from any other meaning, the Church is always described as continuing the life and work of Jesus as Christ dwelling in us and we in Christ. If Christ is alive, that is what Christianity is all about. And, if not, then, though we be of all men the most miserable, the time would have come to wind up the Church in all honesty, and we would be the heirs of two thousand years of make-believe.

But the conviction of Christians is that Jesus is Life, is still continuing. His work is at the beginning: it continues in us. A risen Christ acts only through people. At this time and in this age he has no hands on earth except our hands, no voice but our voice, no means of transformation of the world but in the minds and bodies of his people who are, in every sense except the literal sense, his body.

But the work he began, the redemption of humanity, its transformation, its conversion, he carries on only through us or others. This is not to say that he ever tells us what to do, or very seldom. Of all the theological doctrines, it seems to me that only two are empirically certain. The one is that God is a liberal in the sense that no warning sound from heaven can be expected when we err. He expects us to work our own solution, to select our own occupation and priorities in the light of his known personality, and in the light of what we feel or think about him.

And the other empirically certain doctrine is our capacity for fouling our own nest, breaking our own toys, hurting one another and ourselves, surrounding ourselves with squalor of our own creation. And if I were to call the first doctrine free-will, and the second original sin, I would be doing no more than to describe things by their proper names.

But there are two cognate points that I would seek to add. The first is that the more we succeed in working out our own solutions and in deciding the proper priorities the more we become like Christ, the more we become like ourselves, and perhaps the less we shall resemble one another. If Christ's were simply a human personality this would be a paradox, perhaps even an impossibility. But Christ does not make a poet out of a politician, or a politician out of an engineer, or a philosopher out of a soldier, or a plumber out of a philosopher—that is unless that is what those personalities really need to become. The idea that seeking to be Christ-like we move into a uniformity with one another, is the precise opposite of the truth. This is surely because Christ's personality is divine as well as human and we, because we are only human, can imitate him only by being more perfectly ourselves.

And so it is also true, surely, that he does not intend us even to think alike. The notion that error has no rights;

that truth can be stated for all time in a single set of unalterable propositions, belongs to a pre-scientific view of reality and of human knowledge. Truth is a thing we obtain by dialectics, and dialectic is impossible without dialogue. And so the idea of a Christian political party, or a Christian policy, or a Christian philosophy, or even of a perfectly articulated series of Christian moral precepts, is contrary to the nature of Christianity. It is false to experience, for the Church is not a natural society based on the law; it is a supernatural society based on love. So 'Living in Christ', the process I have been asked to try to describe, is not a state; it is a pilgrimage. It is the slow and deliberate evolution of our own personality, by allowing Christ to live in us. For that is the Christian experience described in the New Testament as 'dwelling in Christ'. It is also described as, and with equal accuracy, 'Christ dwelling in us'.

I am left at the end with the necessity of an avowal of my own faith, with the inevitable consequences you will note my inability to live up to it rather than the strength which it has given me. For more than thirty years Christ has been the light of my life. Many times I have betrayed, neglected, or denied the Light. But never has the Light deserted or betrayed me. Of course, I think of Christ as a historical character, born and dead two thousand years ago. Of course I look for guidance and knowledge to him, about him, in the Gospels, in the historical context of the ancient world, in the tradition of the Christian community. But more and more have I come to realise that this is not the essence of what I mean when I say that I 'believe' in Christ. It is that I think of him as alive and not dead. I think of him as 'here', as 'present', as 'now', as 'within' and not outside the field of my own consciousness, and not as remote in time or space. In other words, in the beautiful phrase of the Greek Orthodox tradition, when I leave the service on Easter Sunday morning I can say with sincerity 'Christ is Risen' and the answer one repeats is that 'He is Risen indeed'.

MRS. EVANS
A PERSONAL STATEMENT

Mrs. Evans, wife of a retired trader in an industrial town in the Coventry diocese.

I am very fortunate to have been born into a Christian family where Christ and his Church were always first in the home, and where the seed of faith was planted and nourished from an early age and which is still growing. I shall always remember my parents with deep gratitude for the fine example they gave to me. But do not imagine that this makes one immune from the temptations and trials of this world; but it does give great strength to overcome them. It is not easy to hurt a friend you love very much, and when I think of the great love of our Lord for us the guilt of offending him is multiplied. He foresaw our difficulties and left us the most wonderful gift, the gift of himself in the eucharist.

The graces this sacrament have given to me are beyond compare. Dare I say that, when I partake of this heavenly food, I feel I know just a little of how St. Paul must have felt when he said: 'It is no longer I who live; but Christ my Lord who lives in me.'

In moments of temptation, in moments of decision, in moments of joy and in moments of sadness, just knowing his hand is there to guide and to strengthen is enough. My husband and I have experienced this 'power beyond ourselves' so many times during our life together. But one incident will always be vivid in our mind. Two years ago, when our eldest son was just sixteen, he developed a disease and his life was in great danger. At the time of crisis we prayed with such faith that God would restore our son to us, just as he gave a son back to a mother when he was on earth. And as we knelt we experienced the strange sensation—difficult to explain—but we knew that the Holy Spirit was near to us and that our prayers would be answered. And so they were. The immediate danger passed, and in time our son was restored to health again. We thanked God for his doctor, who knew how to use his skills, for the nurses who tended him so lovingly and for our vicar who prayed with us and comforted us with the words of St. Paul to the Romans: 'Everything works together for good to those who love God', and for the many friends, new and old who helped us with their prayers.

During these months of preparation for this Call to Mission—and I know I can speak for many—we have lived with Christ. The quiet days of prayer, the wonderful torch processions and the vigils, the lectures and instructions, have brought us so close to him. And the joy when we can help in the little way of bringing another soul to Christ.

The Ninth Talk
LEARN TO LIVE IN CHRIST

Our theme is learning to live in Christ. And the first point I want to make is if we are going to live in Christ, we must admit him into our life. He stands at the door and knocks. He will never force his way in. And, of course, it is possible to keep him outside our whole life. But if we open the door then he comes in. But there is a cost—a twofold cost. When we do ask Jesus he makes us face our sins. It is almost frightening when his eyes expose those dark corners where we know that the baser elements of our personalities lurk. And yet we cannot have love in our lives without that light of love exposing the darkness which is in them. Christ brings with him also the demands of love, revealing our lovelessness and causing us to love. And, the fact is, love is always costly. If we are going then, to invite Christ into our life we must know very clearly who it is whom we thus invite in. There are three Christs, really. There is the Christ of Galilee. I would call him the neighbourhood Christ, the person whom people came to know in his early life, the homely carpenter of Nazareth. This is a wonderful Christ, approachable, intimate, relatively simple of comprehension. He is the only Christ who some people ever know, because they fail to recognise that there is anything more. But there is. Beyond this neighbourhood Christ, there is a mysterious Christ, the awe-inspiring, almost terrible Christ, as revealed on the Mount of Transfiguration, as revealed in the Garden of Gethsemene, when those who came to arrest him fell back, because his full glory shone through. There is the Christ who is saluted by the strange title 'King of Kings, and Lord of Lords'. This Christ so wonderfully described by the author of the fourth Gospel is summed up in the words: 'In the beginning was the Word, and the Word was with God, and the Word was God, the same was in the beginning with God, all things were made by him, without him was not anything made, that was made; in him was life, and the life was the light of men.'

And the great thing to remember is that the neighbourhood Christ and the mysterious Christ are one and the same. But there is the third Christ, combining both those two elements—the Christ who calls us now, one by one, into his service.

When we ask the Christ into our lives, he will not make life easy, as I have said, and will say again. It will not be an escape from life. The Christ, the Lord of love, will take us out into the midst of the battle and danger of this great and thrilling world. And if we ask Christ in, how do we keep him there and how does he keep us there in him? Firstly, by the imitation of Christ in home and daily life we keep him close to our hearts. What is his way of life? It is the way of sacrificial love. Let each one of us take a long hard look at the people we live with and at our relationships with them. Do we demonstrate love? It has been said that a man can be a saint to everybody except in his own home. People can be devils at home and saints outside, and that simply isn't good enough. What does your home look like to Jesus? Is it a happy place? Is it a united place? Is it a Christ-centred place? Let us ensure that our home is an unselfish home, where we make daily and deliberate attempts to replace selfish thinking with thinking for others. And let us ensure that our home is a praying home, a home where there is regular prayer and, if possible, family prayer. It is said: 'The family that prays together, stays together.' Does your family pray together?

And then, we need to have a welcoming home. Let us be sure that our home has the ever-open door and is one which makes time for people. I had a shock, many years ago, if I may be personal, when I discovered that our maid had gone to another priest when she was in trouble. Indeed, I can remember the shock of that still, as you can see from my telling you this. When I asked why she had not come to me, she said: 'Well, I didn't think you'd have time.' A clergyman friend of mine was out one day and his wife answered the phone. Their little son heard her say: 'I'm afraid you must make an appointment with the vicar.' An hour later the child went up to his father and said in his own childish way words to the effect that: 'I want to make an appointment with you.' My friend saw at once that something was seriously wrong with his life when his own child had to come to him in that manner. And yet how easily we can give people the impression that we haven't time, that we must pass on from them to the next task, and so forth. This is particularly disastrous in our own domestic relations, which should be loving and patient. And so I ask again; is *your* home a welcoming home?

It should also be a positive home. How negative we can become, always seeing the worst in people! Somebody once said: 'If you can't say anything good, then don't say anything at all.' When you come back from a holiday people say: 'You do look brown', because you have been exposed to the sun. Similarly, we need to be exposed day by day to Christ, so that people may recognise that fact when they encounter us. And so the first step in keeping Jesus in our life is, very simply, to make time to be with him, and that will involve moments of deliberate recollection before we answer the phone, for example, before we interview or encounter people, before we write to people, and always, before these encounters, we should ask that Christ would give us quietness, and patience, and love in our hearts, and consideration for others.

The second step in this programme of living in Christ is to set aside time for our prayers every day. There is no satisfying relationship, nor ever can be, between two people unless they can talk and listen to each other. And the deeper our friendship, the less we need to speak. So with prayer. The further we go in the life of prayer, the less we need to talk, We begin to listen more. What a lot of time Jesus devoted to prayer! We also must set aside a time and a place. But we can pray in many places. Brother Lawrence prayed in the kitchen, among the pots and pans. I know a business man at this moment who has to go up to London each day, and who has set aside a time for prayer between two service stations on the motorway. I regard that as in the very highest Christian devotional tradition.

The third step in this programme of living in Christ is to read the Bible every day. This is not so easy as it sounds. The Bible is a library of books and it should be read a little at a time, often. People sometimes ask me where they should begin to read the Bible, and I always advise them to begin with the Book of the Acts because there we are introduced to a revolutionary fellowship of adventurous people. It is a logical step to ask ourselves what lies behind that revolutionary fellowship which we read of there, and that will take us to the Gospels for the answer because there we shall meet Christ. And it is a further logical development from that to want to know who he was, and what is the theology and thinking behind the development of the Church since New Testament times. This will take us to the Epistles and these in their turn will lead to the need to ask, if we are moved to want to know, as by this time we shall inevitably be, how it all began, and that will take us to the roots of Christianity, which are deeply embedded in the Old Testament itself. And that, in my view, is the order for anybody who first reads the Bible— the Book of the Acts, the Gospels, the Epistles, and then the Old Testament. And all should be done with a suitable guide, because the Bible is complex and involved and covers such an enormous area of ground that there are few who can find the way across it constructively without, as I have said, a guide.

The fourth step in this four-fold plan of living in Christ is to give personal service and witness to our neighbours and community in the name of Christ himself. There can be no such person as a Christian concerned only with himself. We must always remember the command: 'Bear ye one another's burdens and so fulfil the law of Christ.' Many years ago a famous bishop of Zanzibar, Bishop Frank Weston, said in a meeting in the Albert Hall: 'It is folly, it is madness, to worship Christ in the blessed sacrament and yet to be indifferent to the sufferings of God's creatures.' That was a long time ago; but it is equally true today. It is folly, it is madness; I would put it more strongly and say that it is blasphemy, to try to live with Christ and yet be indifferent to the needs of our neighbours. It is a matter for the deepest thankfulness that this truth is being increasingly recognised by the Church today with its emphasis on Christ the servant, Christ the man for others. And so we are called not just to be part of a worshipping Church, but to be part of a servant Church. And if we are willing to be shown what forms of service to do, the Lord will show us where we are to go, what we are to become, what we are to say, to whom we are to go.

To summarise, there are four steps in asking Jesus to remain with us. First, to learn to imitate him in home and daily life; second, to pray regularly in a set time and place every day; third, to read the Bible carefully and regularly; fourth, to give personal witness and service to the community in the name of the Lord.

Simple? Yes, in a way. But difficult also, because the

lures of the world, the flesh and the devil are very strong. All around us there are distractions and the constant pressure of the idea that it is somehow wrong, or at any rate unsophisticated, to be deeply committed to any cause.

Yet we cannot pull ourselves up by our own bootlaces, as was said long ago. We cannot work our own passage into the Kingdom of Heaven. We cannot earn forgiveness, or merit salvation. All these things were the gifts of God. As Paul put it: 'I'm not ashamed of the gospel of Christ, for it is the power of God, unto salvation, to everyone who believes.'

This salvation, this acceptance by God of us just as we are, unworthy though we are, is focussed in the death of Christ, for there supremely he gives us the power to die to self, to live for him and for others. We cannot do it alone; but he can through us. If the Church is weak today, it is because the Gospel is not being preached. The Gospel is the good news that, as we stand there by the cross, humble, penitent, empty, we find his strength, his grace, his forgiveness, his power. I know this because I have experienced it, and I go on experiencing it again and again. When I am at the end of my tether, the Lord comes to me and says that all that he has is mine: that his grace is sufficient for me; that his strength is made perfect in my weakness. Christ is not merely an example. He is the person to live with, the person who will make our lives wonderfully different and useful. He is all these things but, above all, he is the power unto salvation, who stands before every one of us and says that he offers us forgiveness and power: forgiveness for the dull, inadequate, selfish, lazy, useless lives that have been ours in the past, and offers us power to live an entirely different quality of life. The question is, will we take this offer? Remember the words: 'Behold,

I stand at the door and knock. If any man opens I will come in and make my abode with him.'

I believe as I look at this great crowd that some of you have been deeply moved and challenged by these meetings, and I think you divide into three groups. First, there are those who have been practising Christians for many years, but who would welcome an opportunity of rededicating your life in Christ's service. Second, there are some who have been moved by God to want to commit themselves to Jesus Christ for the first time. Third, there are those who wish to serve God through some vocation, and who may wish to talk over what is involved and to find a way forward. To all of you in those three groups I suggest that you stay behind at the close of the meeting and, when everybody begins to move, that you come forward to the front so that together we can do our business with God. We will pray together a prayer of dedication or rededication, in which you will give your life to Jesus Christ and accept him as your saviour and your Lord and, if you wish, you can talk with somebody who can help you forward in this life of a committed Christian.

* * *

NIGHT 10
MR. COLIN COWDREY

Colin Cowdrey, the famous Kent and England cricketer, was interviewed by Ronald Allison. After some discussion of contemporary issues in cricket, Mr. Cowdrey was asked whether his Christian faith was 'rather academic' or whether it was something which played a great part in his life. He replied: ' I think it might have been academic, and it was in danger of being so because I was brought up in a fine Christian home. It was very easy for me to go to church or not to go to church, as I desired, and most of the family went, and I followed along. Fortunately, it was God's plan that I should move on a little, provoked into thinking a little further and, through my cricket, coming under pressures and strains and tensions which perhaps I wouldn't have had to face in a more hum-drum, day-to-day type of life. I think it was under these strains and pressures that I discovered that I had not sufficient strength in myself to cope, and that I began to think further and grasp for the vital strength that there is.'

As to prayer, Mr. Cowdrey said: 'I try to pray, but in a fully stretched life with so many calls, I have found it difficult to make time. This is the biggest failing probably that I have—to make time for prayer. When I do make time, just to be quiet and pray, I am at once humbled and immediately strengthened, and I think that my greatest wish in life is that I should be able to find and make time. . . . I think the great comfort of the Christian faith is the way that doors open and doors close in a fully committed life. This is the pattern I have learnt to hold for living. You come to crises, a choice of ways in the road, you have a decision to make, and in one's own strength one doesn't know. And then through faith, through prayer, a door closes and another door opens. Maybe one is not very sure at the moment; but on looking back at a later date one can see the working of the spirit and how wonderful it has been. These are rich experiences which keep one going through the dry spells of doubt which assail us all.

MR. JOHN HAYNES
A PERSONAL STATEMENT

John Haynes, a professional advertising agent, was Publicity Executive for the Coventry Call to Mission. Confirmed as an adult, he came into new life in the preparations for the mission, and this was dramatically spoken of in his personal statement.

I want to tell you how looking after the publicity for this mission has changed and deepened my own belief in Jesus Christ. I had become a full member of the Church rather later than most, being baptised and confirmed as an adult, and I attended Church fairly regularly. I knew that when I was asked to help here that I wanted to do the job very much indeed, not just because it looked as if it would be an interesting and a challenging one, but because I was a Christian. But what I didn't know was that before the job was half complete, I would find my own Christian belief changed and strengthened to a real and complete conviction in the power and love of Christ.

After the plans for the mission had been completed, the executive team embarked on a series of meetings of all various parish agents, and it was really at those meetings that I felt, for the first time, the electrifying experience of Jesus Christ at work in people. I don't mean there was a great voice from the sky; but just a certainty and conviction of power and presence. I saw for the first time, too, what Christ at work in people really meant. I think I realised, too, my own commitment to Christ fell very short of what it ought to be. I had gone to those meetings to enthuse the men and women there about working for our Lord, and I realised that they had enthused me!

I came away a different Christian and yet with still some deep reservations about a full commitment.

I am a professional advertising man, and a business man, and I've spent a lot of time making commercial decisions, thinking through other people's problems to find a right way to present their products or services. It's a peculiar business. The advertising world is tough and cynical and needs an attitude of mind that makes one question every action and motive. I think I found this a great stumbling block to my own commitment. The unknown results of such a step, and its possible effect upon my life, conspired to hold me back from what I knew I really wanted to do. It was after those meetings that I became, like many of you, a full time wearer of the badge of the Cross of Nails (the badge of this mission)—a man who advertised that he had belief in Christ. I've worn it ever since in many different places, and it's strange the reaction it produces. Here in the advertising world, not exactly famous for its moral values, is someone who wears a cross, and it has generated a lot of comment, a lot of snide remarks and no small arguments. But principally I think it has made me try to live up to what it represented, and without any doubt it has been a big factor in my change of attitude. It has caused me many times to think twice about a business decision, about people, and about the way I do the job I do.

I was afraid of this full commitment. I sought for reassurance in books to try and qualify and rationalise the feelings I now have. But in all that I have read I am left with the feeling that one reaches a stage at which one must just step over the edge and say 'I believe' and have faith. I believe that through this mission, and through the hundreds of alive Christians that I have met working on it, both within and outside the organisation, that I have been brought personally nearer to Christ. I am sure that my own conviction has been deepened and strengthened by their action and service.

The Tenth Talk
LEARN TO LIVE FOR OTHERS

Now we come to the great theme of learning to live for others. So now, because of a connection between this theme and the greatest of all sacraments, I intend to talk about the Holy Communion. Tomorrow I shall talk about the cross. The two go together, and the reason is this: our normal instinct is for self-preservation—to live for ourselves. We therefore need a powerful counter-influence to live for others. Such a power and such an influence do exist: the power is to be found in the cross, the influence in the Holy Communion.

Christ did not leave behind him any great organisation. He left behind him a meal, which he wanted to be the supreme sacramental way in which we can make and keep contact with him, and he wanted it to hallow all that we do, to be a blessing to all the common things of life; a focus, if you like, in which he blesses and hallows and consecrates the whole of it. And he reminds us in this meal that all life is sacramental, that God is in everything, at the heart and at the root of all that is lovely, creative and true in science, art, commerce, industry, in the whole of life.

We must never forget the Holy Communion Service first took place at the last supper, on the eve of the greatest battle and of the greatest victory in all history. He who was the centre of that supper was in a few hours to become the victim on the cross. The bread and the wine of which we partake in the Lord's supper are the body and blood of the victorious victim, who comes to meet us in this supper with his hands and feet marked with the mark of the nails and his body marked with the mark of the spear. What does he come to give us? He comes to give us the power to live sacrificially, the power to love redemptively; to live and love as he lived and loved. It is fatally easy to forget or to ignore this vitally important meaning of the service. Two books which I have read recently have once again reminded me of this central meaning. The first is *Bury Me In My Boots*, by Sally Trench[1]. I have spoken of this before in these talks more than once, and I have told how, at the age of seventeen, she left her comfortable home to find out how other people live. Her pilgrimage of discovery began among the drug addicts in Piccadilly, and in one of the great London termini. Then she went still deeper. She lived and worked among the meths drinkers who inhabit bombsites in London, not so much speaking about her faith, but living it out in deep compassion by staying alongside them in the name of the Christ in whom she believed and whom she served. Here is a passage from her book:

'For four months I had peformed the ritual of going out and looking for C and every time I had helped him back. Every morning after soup he shuffled out in search of more drink and I knew I would be looking for him again that night. When he left next morning, he never smiled, or said "Thank you", and often I would feel despondent and think that I was wasting my time. And then one day I picked up C and he was very ill. The meths was burning him up fast. I got him back to our

[1] Hodder and Stoughton.

126

shelter and for two days I sat with him as he died. I held his hand, hoping that at one moment or another he would be conscious enough to realise that he was not alone, and that somebody cared. I fed him regularly and bathed down his sweating body and I prayed. When he rallied two days later, I was still there and he knew. His eyes were weak as a result of the meths, and so he couldn't see me, but his grip on my hand tightened. For the first time since I'd known him he smiled and said; "Girl, you're the first person who's ever loved me". I wept many a tear when, a few days later, he died.'

That was her battlefield. Our own may be in our home, where people come with all their needs, lonely, tired, frustrated, mixed-up. Or maybe among our neighbours, where perhaps there is a home where the family is breaking up, or a marriage falling apart, and our help is needed. Or it could be in the office or the factory where we work and in which we may strive to give responsible Christian decisions on important issues. Or it may be that our battlefield will be overseas, wherever there is need and the opportunity of service. Indeed, wherever people are unhappy and lonely, needing to be reconciled in want, deprivation or degradation, there is our battlefield. It could even be that it is amongst people who appear outwardly to be happy and progressive, but need inwardly to be reminded that at the heart of life is God. All this can be summed up in one word—Reconciliation. And that is the heart of the contest and it means two things—putting people right with one another and putting people right with God. The second book I would like to mention was written by a certain Pastor Wurmbrandt: *In God's Underground.*[2] For fourteen years he was in different prisons behind the Iron Curtain. Every night he would try and

[2] Hodder and Stoughton.

get in touch with the man in the next cell by tapping on the walls. A new prisoner arrived and began to answer. He realised that his neighbour was conveying a simple code. 'Who are you?' 'Pastor', he replied. From this cumbersome start, they developed their system. Now I quote from the book:

'He signalled his name. "Bless you" I replied laboriously. "Are you a Christian?" "I cannot claim so." He was a radio engineer awaiting trial on a capital charge, aged fifty-two and in poor health. He had lapsed from faith some years before, having married an unbeliever, and was in deep depression. Before long he tapped: "I would like to confess my sins." It was a confession broken by many silences, and when the man had unburdened things from his heart, he said he felt much happier.'

So these two became what might be called Morse friends, as some other people have become pen friends. The Pastor taught him Bible verses and they exchanged jokes and the Pastor sent him messages about Christ, all in code.

And then one day the Pastor was talking to a young man called Joseph. This was when he was no longer in solitary confinement. Joseph had a disfigured face and was bitter. He was shivering in his shirt, which was threadbare, and the Pastor took his own woollen jacket and persuaded the man to accept it. Joseph's conversion began that day, and yet something was still needed to lift him into faith. It happened during the distribution of the bread ration. One day a surly prisoner tried to cheat the Pastor of his small ration and Joseph was watching. The Pastor told the prisoner: 'Take it, I know how hungry you are.' The prisoner shrugged and stuffed the bread into his mouth, and Joseph watched. That evening Joseph sat translating New Testament verses into English

and suddenly he said: 'Pastor, we've read nearly everything Jesus said, but I still wonder what he was like to
meet as a man.' And the Pastor said: 'I'll tell you,
Joseph', and he began to talk about another man who
had given away everything he had. Pastor Wurmbrandt
ended by saying, 'Jesus is like that.' Joseph said: 'Pastor,
if Jesus is like you and him, then I love Jesus too.' On the
day of his departure, Joseph embraced the Pastor and there
were tears in his eyes as he said: 'You helped me as though
you were my own father. Now at least I can stand by
myself with God.'

Years after they met, they met again and the Pastor
found that he had become a true Christian, no longer
ashamed to bear the scar on his face. Now that is the kind
of warfare to which you and I are called. Obviously, the
circumstances may not be anything like as dramatic as
that. Let us pray God they may not be. But into circumstances of testing and trial the way of the cross is bound
to lead us and along that way and through those battle-
fields the Holy Communion is an essential to it. It is a
battlefield encounter with one who comes to meet us with
the marks of suffering in his body, and calls upon us to
follow him through conflict and beyond.

With this in mind I bring you three vital sentences
from the Communion Service. We may take them with
us from this meeting. The first is this: 'Ye that do truly
and earnestly repent your sins and are in love and charity
with your neighbours, draw near with faith. . .'

At this present moment we have two-and-a-half days
before the great Eucharist on Sunday which will be the
climax of this mission. That means that we have two-and-
a-half days in which to repent us of our sins, in which to
put right those wrong relationships with others which
most of us have, to reconcile ourselves with those whom

we dislike, to ask pardon of those we have hurt by our tongue or by our actions, to ask pardon of those of whom we have been jealous. That is in the name of Christ strive to put these things right: to apologise, to make amends, to make confession, so that we can come to the Holy Communion with a quiet heart and a quiet conscience.

The second sentence is this: 'Draw near with faith and take this holy sacrament to your strengthening.'

That sentence brings us to the very heart of that personal contact with God who is at the heart of all true religion. 'Draw near with faith.' It is not by our merits or by our desserts that we earn God's forgiveness. We do not win our way into the Kingdom of God by our own efforts or our own good work. We enter the Kingdom of God by faith in our Lord's overflowing love portrayed for us upon the cross, and it is with this faith that we approach the holy sacrament. I ask you now: Is your faith this kind of faith? Do you really believe in the love of God revealed in Jesus? Have you ever put your whole trust in Jesus and his quality of love? If not there is something missing in your life. Do you really believe that he believes in you? Simon Peter, that resolute, loyal man, moved forward in his own strength and then came failure, despair, encounter, forgiveness, acceptance, restoration. The Lord accepted him, failure though he was. I ask you, therefore, again, whether you really believe that he, Christ, believes in you? Are you prepared to wager your whole life on this conviction—the belief that, at the heart of life, there is one who believes in you and longs for you to live, not wobble through this life, as Studdert Kennedy used to say. Do you believe that?

The offer of Christ is still available. All we have to do is to accept in faith that he has faith in us, that he died among us, that he still believes in us and that he still goes on believing in us, because he knows that if we will but give him our trust and put our faith in him, then his love and his power will begin to flow into us and through us. 'Draw near with faith, and take this holy sacrament for your strengthening.'

And here is the third and the last sentence: 'Here, O Lord, we offer and present unto thee ourselves, our souls and bodies.'

I think of that as the putting of a bunch of keys upon the altar. To my mind, these are the keys which our Lord wants of us: the key of every room in the house of our life, the key of our money, the key of our friendship, the key of our career, the key of our reputation and of our ambition. He needs us to offer him ourselves with all these keys, not just in our own strength, but in return for all that he has given to us. He needs us to hand these to him in gratitude and to offer him ourselves. He will then give us the strength to fight the battle of reconciliation, to love like people such as Sally Trench and Pastor Wurmbrandt. He will give us the courage not to mind being derided. He will give us the love to love the unlovable, he will give us the ability to go on going on. He wishes us to offer ourselves just as we are, asking only that we should want to be different; that we should want to be his follower, that we should be prepared to be taken by him and to have broken in ourselves all that has hitherto prevented us from this act of total surrender—our fears, our weaknesses, our indolences. Then he will make us wholly his for time and for eternity.

* * *

LORD CARRON

A Roman Catholic and a former president of the Amal-
gamated Engineering Union, and an eminent trade
unionist for many years, Lord Carron spoke on the last
night of the mission before the Bishop gave his final
address on 'Learn to Live for God'.

Many speakers have preceded me in joining the clergy
and people in the diocese of Coventry in the celebration
of this golden jubilee of the re-establishment of this ancient
diocese. All participants have one characteristic which
they share with you and with me—a firm belief in the one
true God, the almighty father of mankind, and in his
divine son, our Lord Jesus Christ. Without that basic
belief, and our recognition of the omnipotence of God,
there is no reason at all for the existence of this or any
other diocese. Divested of that belief, scriptures tell us,
vain is our faith. Whilst it is right and fitting that we should
collectively claim our faith, it is of far greater importance
that we should practice it as individuals in our daily
life.

Most of that will be done quietly, almost surreptitiously,
bearing public witness only as duty and occasion demands.
In that respect I suppose we all tend to regard ourselves
as failures, especially when contemplating the lives of
heroic virtue of those presented to us as examples. Para-
doxically, our very recognition of our failures is, if we continue to persevere, our greatest success, so shall we be
judged.

Time, drawing a partial curtain over history, presents
to us the spiritually attractive characteristics of the great

saints; those who appear almost to walk with God. But their human failings tend to be obscured. Often in an excess of zeal we try to emulate their outstanding virtues, and as often, to our mortification, we fail. At times we become disheartened, not realising that their failures may have been as many and as great as ours. But they persevered. Their trust in God did not waver. Rightly we revere those saintly ones. We are lost in admiration of them, but we so desperately seek an example from those on whom we feel to be on equal terms.

Are there any of us who do not feel not only reverence and admiration, but love, for St. Francis? Why? Is it not because we do know of his imperfections from himself? Is it not because he was so saddened at his failures? But most of all, is it not because of his great love for all God's creatures, his brothers and sisters under the fatherhood of God? Do we not feel that we could have a better chance of some success in our endeavours by setting him as our example, rather than any other?

At least there is one great virtue possessed by Francis which we can all practice. I speak of tolerance. Never was tolerance so required in the daily lives of all of us as it is today. More capable orators with more time than I have at my disposal could, with great skill and conviction, develop the theme. I feel I really do not need to do so. Every one of us could, without any difficulty, give examples of where tolerance should be practised. Unfortunately, it is always the other person who we find deficient. Seldom is it 'I'. Necessarily, tolerance does not mean blind acquiescence in everything. Basic principles cannot be rejected. But even though the effort at times may be great, seeming on occasions to be impossible, nevertheless there is no circumstance that I can think of where this virtue cannot be practised.

Who is more tolerant than God himself? Without his tolerance not one of us would be here tonight. This call to mission would have great significance and would fulfil an objective were it solely the material celebration of the restoration of the diocese. But this call to mission is not intended to have only that objective. The deep down purpose of the mission is to recognise that we are all individually members of God's Church that in fact all human beings are God's children, created in his image and likeness and, as Francis recognised, all brothers and sisters under his divine fatherhood.

We recognise the omnipotence of God, and from this mission we must resolve to live our lives in him, and for him. Could I suggest as a first practical step to those who do not already do so, to make a brief offering each day to God of all one's actions and activities. It is surprising what an effect this almost insignificant action can have. Not that in every minute of the day one is conscious of having made the offering: but it is surprising, and often, in my own experience, very comforting how the recollection flashes across one's mind.

Our imperfections will still persist; but the almighty recognises that we are imperfect human beings, and he does not expect of us more than that of which we are capable. Let us then, each and every one of us, go about our daily activities in his name. If we can all try, and try hard with the help of God, to practice tolerance, then this call to mission will have achieved, I am sure, even more than was hoped.

MR. SANDERS
A PERSONAL STATEMENT

Mr. Sanders, at the time of the mission, was Area Director of the National Coal Board, having lived at Atherstone, a town within the diocese.

Whilst Lord Carron was developing his wide and beneficent influence in trade unionism and in public life, in the humble field and often thankless task of management in industry I was progressing from controlling a handful of men to become the business leader of many thousands, and in my early thrusting years I spent many sleepless nights worrying my way through problems of difficult business and contrary people.

It took me a long time to learn four important lessons. Firstly, that people are always more important than things; secondly that God knows all about the requirements of our everyday lives just as clearly now as when Christ said 'Your father knoweth that you have need of these things.' And thirdly, the quite astounding truth that if a man, as best he knows how, in all parts of his life, seeks first the Kingdom of God, all other needful things are added. Not luxury, maybe, but all reasonable necessities. And fourthly, that the ability and capacity to lead others is a God-given endowment and that the most effective way to command is to serve. This is what Christ meant when he said that he who is first among you must become least. This does not mean becoming weak or servile; or practising a hollow praternalism. Nor is it a form of humanism. To set an example of hard work, integrity, service in a common cause, and genuine care for one's fellow men is the course that many leaders who seek a crown shrink from.

Francis Kerr has put it this way: 'He that has no cross deserves no crown', while Dag Hammarskjold said on the same topic: 'Only he deserves power who every day justifies it.'

I suggest to you that much of our moral sickness in these days stems from the utterly mistaken assumption that in the world of work God's laws are irrelevant and inapplicable, and that in science, industry, business and commerce, God has no place, that he somehow hasn't kept up with modern technology and social change. But how foolish and empty this attitude is; if God can say 'I am the same yesterday, today and tomorrow, and the source of all knowledge' then surely progress from the abacus of A.D. 30 to today's computer only represents the unveiling to man, by God, of an infinitesimal part of the sum total of knowledge. And the same comment is equally true of electronics, of nuclear power, of medicine or of any other field of human endeavour. Where we seem to be failing so miserably is in the realm of human morality. The spiritual development of man falls far short of his material attainment. Men and nations alike are losing their way, partially because they are not properly directed; but also because they worship the false god of materialism and break the very first commandment

Many years ago, Rudyard Kipling gave an address to students at McGill University in Montreal. He was warning students against over-concern for money, or position, or power, and he said: 'Some day you will meet a man who cares for none of these things, and then you will realise how poor you are.'

Have not most of us met some such saintly man or woman and seen in them a quality of life which arouses our deepest wonder and admiration? Momentarily we catch a glimpse of a richness of life in such people we would dearly love to emulate. And then, so often, family and place, duty and conditions, reassert their grip, the glow fades, and becomes as misty as a dream. So often God knocks at the door of our lives in the strangest places and circumstances, bringing wonder and uplift of spirit to a point almost beyond man's understanding. Equally often we do not recognise God's voice and therefore fail to say yes to his invitation to allow him to inject into our lives new purpose, new meaning and new power.

Such invitation I feel sure has been extended to many people during this memorable Call to Mission, particularly in this Cathedral during the last two weeks. How many, I wonder, will accept? I know that from the hour when I said 'yes' I became certain that existence is meaningful and that my life, in surrender, had purpose: not purpose that I can always see as clearly as I would wish; but purpose that daily unfolds as one steps out in faith.

I know only too well the lonely burden of industrial leadership. And that, without God's never-failing help, the right wife, and a home which is a haven, the sheer load of living can become almost unbearable. Yet my wife and I have proved the complete truth of the admirable words of the late King George VI in his Christmas message of 1939, as some of you may remember. He said this: 'I said to the man who stood at the gate of the year, give me a light that I may tread safely into the unknown, and he replied, go out into the darkness and put your hand into the hand of God; that shall be better to you than light, and safer than the known way.' And this is the only way that I know to 'Learn to live for God'.

The Eleventh Talk
LEARN TO LIVE FOR GOD

As we come to the end of this testing and searching adventure into faith, we come face to face with the most fundamental duty of all—learning to live for God. It is a sober fact that we live in a generation which, although it may still believe in God's existence, is perhaps more bent on excluding him from life than any previous one in history. The idea that God is dead is not merely a theological catch-phrase; but a conviction, even if subconsciously held, of thousands of people who live as though he does not exist. For the majority God scarcely enters into their daily habits or outlooks. This is certainly true of the world in its technological aspect, in which man is finding that he can control and manipulate areas of matter to an extent undreamt of by previous generations. One consequence is that, instead of seeing God in all, he assumes that man is the creator and not merely the discoverer.

It is true that man can live without God. But it must be said that he can also live without love; he can live without compassion; he can live without mercy. But what kind of life would this be? It is God that gives colour and life and truth to our existence. It follows that the supreme action any of us can do in this life is to witness to the reality of God. But first we must ask ourselves what and who is this God to whose reality we are to witness, and whose wonder we are to worship. The answer to both those questions lies in the cross of Christ. The cross, as a cosmic event in history, was inevitable. It represents, all through the ages, a clash between two different philosophies of life. It represents the clash between the materialist outlook on life which has at its heart the conviction that this earthly existence of ours is all there is. It is a dead and hopeless creed. Shakespeare has expressed it marvellously: 'The cloud-capp'd towers, the gorgeous palaces, the solemn temples, the great globe itself, yea, all which it inherit shall dissolve and, like this insubstantial pageant faded, leave not a rack behind. We are such stuff as dreams are made on, and our little life is rounded with a sleep.'

Such is the poetic expression of the matter. Much less poetic is the fact that this earthbound, as it were, materialist idea of this life as all that is, leads inevitably to a philosophy which is essentially selfish. If the material things of life are all that matter, it follows inevitably that men do all in their power to acquire as many of them as possible while yet there is time. Sooner or later that way of life is bound to come into conflict with the way of life laid down by Jesus. We who try to follow the way of Christ—and I pray that there will be many of us after this mission—must be prepared for conflict with this outlook.

But, after all, there is always bound to be conflict for the Christian, as there was at Calvary, for Christ. On the one side there are those whose basic purpose is destruction, on the other side is the Christ who said: 'Love your enemies, do good to them that hate you, bless them that curse you, pray for them that do spitefully use you, and to him that smites you on the other cheek, offer the other, to him that takes your cloak away forbid not to take your coat also. Give to every man that asks of you and of him that takes away your goods do not ask them again. Love your enemies, do good, be merciful, as your father in heaven is merciful.'

And the cross is inevitable because it involves going across the road, as it were. Love does not stand on safe ground offering good advice. Love goes across the road where there is danger and need. The material world, with all its iron-clad ideas, will resist such a way of life as it resisted that way of life in Christ. So long as the Church, which represents Christ, stands apart there is no opposition. But where the Church preaches the Gospel and still more where the Church lives the Gospel, then the world will hit back.

Who is on that Cross? Here is God, supremely at work on that cross. Here is love, loving. Unless we see this, we can all too easily worship a false God, an angry God, a sentimental God, a disinterested God. But there on the Cross is the true nature of God revealed. Here is God saying in and through Jesus: 'I am the way'—the only way to live, the way of self-giving love. 'I am the truth'—the truth that he who tries to save his life will lose it, but he who is prepared to throw it away will find it. 'I am the life'—the life worth living, abundant life. Nobody can pressurise a person into an awareness of, or a response to, the cross. Every person must find his own way to that place. But to each committed Christian there comes the moment when, looking at Jesus on the Cross he says, 'Thou art the Christ'.

What did God do on that cross? He united. He united man with God and men with one another; even the very manner of his dying demonstrates this. How can one hate in the presence of such a love? Here is a work of reconciliation, here is love in action.

You and I are called upon to do three things in reaction to this cross. We are to look up at it, we are to look out at the world from behind it, and we are to go out into the world from in front of it. As we look up at the cross we realise that we put him there. We put him there by our compromises, our worldliness, our timidities, our lack of decisiveness in his service and of commitment to his person.

And as we look up at that cross we realise that he still loves us. Despite all that we have done to him, God still loves us. Despite our inadequacy, our indifference, our compromises, he still goes on loving. Let me speak personally here. Forty years ago I discovered on that cross a love that would not let me go, a love that would not let me down by playing down the gravity of my sins and failures, and a love that would not let me off the penalty of judgment. But above all I found myself lifted up into a new understanding of what life could be like in the presence and the forgiveness and the power of God.

What happens when we look out on the world from behind the cross? I have very rarely heard this suggested; but it is important, to stand behind that cross and to look out on the world with the eyes of Jesus, those eyes that noticed the little woman in the crowd, the dwarf up the tree, the woman at the well, and the mother who had lost her boy. When we begin to do this there begins to well up within us a great longing to go out into this suffering, fallen, unhappy world with the message of love so clearly portrayed on that Cross.

What happens when we go out from that cross into the world? That is what the real Christians have done, all down the centuries. A half-converted person goes around in a false glow of supposed devotion; but the truly converted witness in dynamic love and service in the power of sin forgiven through Christ.

And so I come to the last thought I wish to share with you as we stand at the foot of the cross. It is this: what are you and I called upon to do by that figure on the cross? We are called to love, to heal, and to reconcile, as I have all along been trying to say. We're being called to love even the unloving, and certainly the unlovable and unloved. We are being called to a love that knows no limits in response to a love that has shown no limits. We are being called to heal, in the sense of making men whole, because man is composed of body and mind and soul, and to attempt to heal the body without the mind and soul is utterly inadequate. In this work of healing we are being called to listen with one ear to God and one ear to the person in need, and to bring, through God, total healing.

And we are called, especially, to reconcile. We are called to unite man with man, and man with God; to allow him to bring peace to them that are afar off and to them that are near, which means, to bring peace among races, peace among the nations, peace in our homes and peace in our hearts. By all means within our power, never being discouraged by any sense at any time of the smallness of what we may be able to achieve in the limited areas of our personal lives.

As we come to the end of this Call to Mission, let it not be an end but a new beginning. For myself, I would like to end by reading the words on a card which will be available to all those of you who wish, by receiving one, to have a permanent reminder of what you have under-taken to do as a consequence of all that has happened here. The words are these: 'During this Call to Mission I have learned more deeply what it means to be alive unto God. I have seen more clearly what he has done for me and for the world through Jesus Christ. In response I desire to dedicate myself to the service of my Lord, and in this spirit of gratitude I pledge myself to read my Bible every day, to share fully in the worship, life and fellow-ship of the Church; to be loyal to Jesus by word and deed and to serve him at home, at work and in the world.'

May that card become a daily reminder of a covenant made with God by you, a covenant in which you have accep-ted Jesus as Saviour and Lord, and have agreed to commit your life to him and to serve him with your will and your mind and your heart, wherever he may ask you to serve him.

4

The Continuing Task

THE CALL to Mission was part of a carefully arranged programme to celebrate the fiftieth anniversary of the refounding of the ancient diocese of Coventry. Four separate events were planned, and it seems proper, here at the end of a book which has been concerned principally with one of them, just to recapitulate what they were. First, a large-scale missionary exhibition was arranged, designed to help the church recognise its part in the world-wide family of churches, and to help us all to turn our eyes away from our purely domestic and local affairs. It was designed also to stir up vocations to the work of the Church overseas. This exhibition was held for ten days in Coventry Cathedral and attracted over ten thousand people. The second event to be held was a conference called 'People and Cities', which was a very large-scale enterprise designed, with the help of experts from many lands, to study man sociologically in his emerging social environment. This ambitious and highly successful project owed very much to the inspiration and leadership of Canon Stephen Verney.

The third part of the programme was the Call to Mission, with which this book has largely been concerned although, as I trust has been made abundantly clear, this itself was but part of a larger whole. Its purpose was to deepen the spiritual life of the people of the diocese and to enable all of us to look out with purpose and greater sense of responsibility for the lives of those many thousands who have little use for the Church. The fourth part of the programme was a gathering, as has already been stated, of almost the whole Christian family of the diocese, in a great and ever-memorable eucharist, held in the open air, at the end of the Call to Mission. This was held on the Feast of St. Michael and All Angels, the exact day of the anniversary of the refounding of the diocese, and is a date and an occasion which will surely not fade from the memories of those who experienced it. Thirteen thousand people attended.

Now that all these four important events belong to the past, the important question to ask concerns the following-up, the continuing task of seeing that the work begun goes on and bears fruit. The Call to Mission must be seen as part of the on-going mission of the Church: indeed it will always seem as such. This on-going mission must, of necessity, continue largely in the parochial life of the Church. The actual Call to Mission was never seen as an end in itself; as an isolated event. So the last night of the actual mission marked in fact the beginning of this on-going task, to which the whole diocese was and is committed.

With this in mind I made it clear from the outset of the planning of the Call to Mission that the most important part of the mission would be, in fact, in the follow-up. We therefore laid careful plans for it. This was done firstly, with regard to the clergy, secondly with regard to the laity. For the clergy, a conference was held at Keele University in the year following the Call to Mission itself, just after Easter. Four main topics were discussed; theological, sociological, evangelistic, and what might be called the exercise and development of the spiritual life.

To help us in our thinking, four speakers were invited

to address the conference—Father John Coventry, S.J. came over from Heythrop to lecture to the clergy on recent theological developments. His two lectures were much appreciated and have led to discussion groups and training courses. A whole-time officer for adult religious education has been appointed, a part of whose work will be the arranging of study courses for the clergy, who will have an opportunity to go more deeply into recent theological developments during the past few years. The second speaker was Archbishop Anthony Bloom who gave three lectures on the life of prayer and spirituality in general. We hope that these lectures will also be followed up by clergy desirous to come together to learn more about prayer and education. The third lecture was by a Pentecostalist minister, the Rev. W. T. H. Richards, from Slough, who laid before us some basic principles of effective evangelism. Since then, courses have been arranged for clergy who desire to discover together how they can more effectively bring people into a 'living experience of the love and forgiveness of our Lord Jesus Christ', and how they can 'bring people alive unto God'. I think that most of us clergy would feel that we are inadequate in this difficult but all-important task of bringing people into a living relationship with God.

The fourth speaker was the Dean of Liverpool, the Very Rev. Edward Patey, who spoke to us about the Church in relation to the community, pointing out that clergy still have an important part to play in the social out-reach of the Gospel. His lecture is being effectively followed up by a series of study courses, arranged by Canon Stephen Verney.

With regard to the laity meetings have been held for those whose lives were deepened by the Call to Mission. Several hundreds came to these meetings and all who spoke expressed profound gratitude for what Call to Mission had meant, not only to them but to their parish and to the diocese. A number of laity spoke, giving their own personal testimony to what the mission had meant to them, and a large number expressed keenness to enter into further training in evangelism and spirituality, sociology and theology. A whole-time officer, the Rev. Alan Boddington has been appointed to arrange courses of study, week-end training courses, to visit the parishes, and to keep in touch with those whose lives were changed or deepened by the Call to Mission.

I thought that it might be of interest to include in this narrative the stories of a few whose lives were enriched as a result of the Call to Mission. And here indeed are some instances with which Mr. Boddington has been good enough to supply me.

1. A boy at an Approved School. One of the Diocesan Readers counselled a young man at one of the mission meetings and kept in touch with him afterwards. He was at an Approved School in the area. The young man told his friends about his new-found faith and they beat him up in return. The Reader, however, kept up his visits to the school and later the young man was prepared for confirmation.

2. A number of men have come forward to serve as Readers because of the mission. One man, the manager of a colliery, had been to train as a Counsellor at the training sessions held by Canon Rogers. At one of the very early mission meetings he spoke to the Chief Counsellor at one of the centres at the end of the meeting. He said: 'Although I am a Counsellor, I am myself in need of counsel. What is God saying to me?' It turned out, after talking things over with a number of people, that God was asking for a far deeper commitment of his life, and this

146

has resulted in training to be a Reader and increased activity in his own parish in a number of ways.

3. A mother and her son went forward on the last night of the mission in one of the centres. It was essentially an act of repentance, for she bore a heavy burden of guilt due to years of unfaithfulness in her marriage. Later, with her vicar, she talked it all through and received from him the assurance that when we truly repent God really forgives and forgets. Together they knelt at the communion rail confessing their need of, and asking for, Christ's forgiveness. The woman went on her way that day rejoicing in a new-found peace. She is active now in her parish Bible study group, and is a regular worshipper.

4. Bob came to the mission with a friend. I think they met in a pub. He was right outside the Church but was gloriously converted. He just can't read enough about the Christian faith, attends a Bible study group and has been away on several week-ends run by the Diocesan Youth Chaplain.

5. Elizabeth was converted some years ago. After taking part in the Counsellor Training Course she really 'found herself' at the mission meetings, spoke to one of the Counsellors about a deeper dedication to the Lord's service, and since that time has gained greatly in confidence in Christ.

6. Mrs. T was separated from her husband. Before the mission, her parish church visited many of the homes in the area, and she accepted their invitation because she had 'nothing better to do' as she said afterwards. She was converted on the first night. Since the mission she has become greatly involved in Church life, and has taken on the position of Assistant Youth Club Leader. Some months afterwards her small boy was baptised.

7. Many Church people gained enormous confidence, both through the training sessions before the mission and

the meetings themselves. Many now run home meetings or Bible study groups and prayer cells.

8. Andrew now helps in a coffee bar run by a Church Army sister. He often speaks of the Call to Mission as the time when things 'really made sense'.

9. One night the Bishop was speaking about Death—the problems it can leave with the widowed partner. In the Cathedral ruins the Chief Counsellor noticed a woman stop on her way through and listen intently to the whole of the address, standing in the pouring rain. Afterwards, he spoke to her. She just happened to be coming through that way on that particular night, bearing her great sense of loneliness at the recent loss of her husband. Jesus Christ brought her a peace that night that otherwise she might never have found.

10. A lady had two tickets for a mission meeting. At the very last moment she had a phone call to say that her friend could not make it. On the way to the Cathedral she wondered to whom she could give her spare ticket. Standing outside there was a coloured nurse, and after offering her the ticket, they went in together. For the next four nights they went together. At first the nurse said it was 'so much more worth-while than other ways of spending an evening'. On the fifth night she went forward and gave her life to Jesus Christ.

Such, as I have said, are some of the events which have happened during all the long stretch of time which has now elapsed since those nights of mission. This continuing task continues, and it is possible now, after such a lapse of time, to say that it continues fruitfully.

I realise only too clearly that many mistakes in the preparation for the Call to Mission were made, that it could have been far more effective than it was; I realise also that the follow-up has not been what it might have been. But, having said all that, I have no doubt in my mind that the Call to Mission has made a profound impact upon very many people. Furthermore, I believe that unless the Church is powerful in evangelism, the Church will die. Other people may express their evangelism in many different ways from the Call to Mission that was held in this diocese; that there needs to be in the Church as a whole a far greater emphasis upon evangelism I have no doubt whatever.

It is sometimes said by critics that the day of 'missions' is over. This may or may not be true. But of one thing I am quite certain, that the day of mission will never be over. The Church lives or dies in accordance with its willingness to go out in mission to the great un-churched masses who appear to live as though there were no God, and whose values have been but little affected by the life and teaching of Christ. Our task must always be not merely to look after those who are within the worshipping community of the Church, but it must be deeply concerned with those who have little use for the Christian message and the Christian ethic. Insofar as we are planning for these people, insofar as we are seeking to reach them by every possible means, only so will the Church be said to be alive and effective. In this diocese we have at least been conscious of our need to go out in the name of Christ to the great masses of people who appear to have very little use for the Church. Although the numbers of those people who came to the mission may have been limited, (it was, in fact, of the order of forty thousand) nevertheless the fact is that many who did come were deepened in their allegiance to Christ and given a fresh dynamic, so to live and pray, to think and worship and witness, that they will not cease in their task, but proclaiming by their life, their deed and their word their gratitude to the sustaining love of our Lord.